"BREEZY ...
CHELSEA is not o   e
possibilities of a dog-   -
opening journey into the deaf subculture as well."
—*The Oakland Tribune*

"Paul Ogden's book is a loving tribute to one of man's (and woman's) most loyal and best friends—the dog. Though the book delves into the barriers that deaf people face in their daily lives, the author refuses to create sympathy or portray deaf people as victims. Instead, he brings forth a touching portrait of two ordinary people whose lives are touched by a very special friend—a pet whose talents help them realize what most of us take for granted every day. CHELSEA: THE STORY OF A SIGNAL DOG has meaning for anyone who has loved a pet."
—MARLEE MATLIN

"God bless the Chelseas of this world for making it a better place. The book is a delight and I loved every page."
—BETTY WHITE

"Some people who relate personal experiences are unsure how to create the right emotion. . . . Ogden is not ambiguous. Nor is he cold or impersonal. He just tells about his feelings the same way he lives. Direct. No background noise and no detours. And he does it gently with touches of compassion and humor. . . . The facts about how remarkable Chelsea really is are better than fiction because Ogden tells only what he sees."
—Associated Press

Also by Paul Ogden:

THE SILENT GARDEN: Understanding the
  Hearing Impaired Child (with Suzanne Lipsett)

CHELSEA

The Story of a Signal Dog

Paul Ogden

FAWCETT CREST • NEW YORK

Sale of this book without a front cover may be unauthorized. If this book is coverless, it may have been reported to the publisher as "unsold or destroyed" and neither the author nor the publisher may have received payment for it.

A Fawcett Crest Book
Published by Ballantine Books
Copyright © 1992 by Paul W. Ogden

All rights reserved under International and Pan-American Copyright Conventions. Published in the United States by Ballantine Books, a division of Random House, Inc., New York, and simultaneously in Canada by Random House of Canada Limited, Toronto.

No part of this book may be reproduced in any form or by any electronic or mechanical means, including information storage and retrieval systems, without permission in writing from the publisher, except by a reviewer who may quote brief passages in a review.

Letter from "Dear Abby" column used with permission of Abigail Van Buren.

Library of Congress Catalog Card Number: 91-20928

ISBN 0-449-22200-4

This edition reprinted by arrangement with Little, Brown and Company, Inc.

Manufactured in the United States of America

First Ballantine Books Edition: August 1993

Cover photo by G. Paul Bishop

This book is decicated to
Anne Keenan Ogden, who once said,

"I never dreamed that I could possibly love a dog
until I met my husband, Paul."

Acknowledgments

CHELSEA'S book is very much a dog story and is meant to appeal to dog lovers the world over. In addition, in a humorous and unobstructive way, it is also a book about deafness. The daily life of a deaf family comes through from beneath the surface of what is first and foremost the story of a dog.

My warmest thanks go to the many people who helped me with the book project, all of them definitely dog lovers: Carolyn Anderson, Steve and Nancy Bock, Nancy Mitchell Carroll, Linda Hammer-Brown, Pamela Howard, Jill Maled, Tom and Mary Betty Rule, Susan Rutherford, Renée Souleret, Pamela J. Warkentin, Kathy Yoshida.

Special appreciation goes to the following people: Kaye Hall, Chelsea's breeder, for donating Chelsea to Canine Companions for Independence in Santa Rosa, California, and for her continuing insights into the personality of Belgian sheepdogs.

Bonita (Bonnie) M. Bergin, Founder and Director of Research at Canine Companions for Independence, for her roles as expert matchmaker and head trainer at the boot camp. After fifteen years as the executive director, she has taken on a new CCI role in order to focus on research and development, and international public relations.

Pat Stewart and Lisa Merrill, Chelsea's puppy raisers.

Patti Murphy, Kerry Knaus, Mary Allen, and the staff at Canine Companions for Independence, for working with Chelsea and training her.

Faculty, staff, and students at California State University, Fresno, for their support of my writing projects, especially to my colleagues, who are also fond of dogs and even people.

Suzanne Lipsett for her editorial skills and her ear for language.

Dunbar and Annegret Ogden, my brother and his wife, for cheering me on in my writing efforts.

Al Zuckerman for recommending my manuscript to Little, Brown and Company.

Colleen Mohyde, my editor at Little, Brown and Company, for her stimulating ideas, her artistic sensitivity, and for spending part of her honeymoon traveling to meet Chelsea.

Anne Keenan Ogden, my wife and, together with Chelsea, my best friend.

CHAPTER 1

Lox

IT was my last year in graduate school at the University of Illinois in Champaign-Urbana, Illinois, and it was *cold*. I didn't want or need to go out much that winter, since I'd finished all my course work and was working on my dissertation. I lived alone in a comfortable apartment, had most of my research materials stacked in close around me—and several months ago while on a job search on the West Coast I had met the girl I had decided I wanted to marry, although I hadn't yet informed her how she fit into my plans. But she lived two thousand miles away in Long Beach, California, so there wasn't much reason to go out in the cold.

Still, I soon became aware of how very much *alone* I was in my home. I suppose a hearing person might describe that time as a very quiet period. To me, who had been deaf* since birth, the lack of noise wasn't a problem. But except for the vibrations of my own footsteps

---

*The word *deaf* is used in two ways, depending on the user. Professionals such as medical doctors and audiologists use the word to refer to severe hearing loss, as opposed to *hard of hearing*, which can be light to quite serious but is correctable to some extent by hearing aids. People in the deaf community like me, on the other hand, use *deaf* to identify themselves as members of a specific subculture. We are proud of this identification and do not perceive it as a pathological label in any way.

across the floor and the movement of my chair when I pulled it up to my desk in the mornings, the flat was unnaturally still. It was the perfect time, I decided in a moment of inspiration, to get myself a dog.

From my earliest days, dogs had meant home to me in a special way. Home was Charleston, West Virginia, but my parents had sent me to a residential school for the deaf in St. Louis, Missouri, when I was five years old. I went home on holidays and during the summer, and when I had to wrench myself away again and travel to school, my first dog, Happy, stayed in my mind as a symbol of our family feeling. Happy was a pretty little red thing with a pointed nose and bushy tail, and we all chose her name with the idea of cheering me up. It was no accident that Happy resembled a fox. We got her from a farmer who told us a fox had invaded the kennel in which he raised Chihuahuas, and Happy was part of the result. She represented home for me all through my boarding school years, and after Happy died we had other dogs, until I left for college, when my life became too unpredictable to include a dog.

Now, though, I had hit a hiatus—nothing to do but write that dissertation and make it through the long, cold Illinois winter. A dog would add a dash of liveliness to the academic drudgery of analyzing statistics—on the relationship between education and socioeconomic variables—in a sample of deaf adults—and I'd have a chance to really train the dog the way I knew it ought to be trained. I could work on the training all semester, and at the end I'd have a skilled dog when I moved on to the first job of my career in the training of teachers of the deaf. I could even teach the dog to respond to manual signs. Why not? I liked the idea of living with a dog who depended on its eyes for communication as much as I did. I had in mind a puppy who wouldn't have to unlearn a strong dependency on verbal signals.

I had a good friend, Debbie, a hearing woman who worked as an interpreter in some of my graduate classes. She was a proven dog lover, and she had a fabulous husky named Avalanche who was as pure white as—well, yes, the driven snow, with not a trace of another color anywhere except in his black shiny eyes and duller black nose. In my occasional breaks Debbie and Avalanche and I often shared a walk or winter romp of an hour or two, and Debbie was eager for me to get a dog so we could all take our breaks together. Hoping to get in on the selection process for a friend for Avalanche, she went with me to the pound one day in early February to begin my search.

Inside the pound's "cell block," the frigid air had found its way under the little sliding doors to the individual cages and somehow it intensified the terrible odors floating up from the cell floors. I looked at Debbie and her face was squinched up tight; even her eyes were squinting. I realized it wasn't just the smell she was trying to shut out. As we walked down the aisle between two lines of cells, dog after dog ran forward to bark at us, and Debbie was reacting to the din. Deaf people have their own special blessings to count. One is that they're never kept up all night by the barking of a neighbor's dog.

I loved these moments when it was perfectly obvious not just to me but to all the world that deafness, though perhaps not the most convenient condition, was hardly the handicap many people believe it to be. In general, hearing people see the deaf as seriously disabled if not downright deficient. They are always surprised to learn—and have trouble believing—that deaf people see themselves as healthy and normal and sometimes, as now, even lucky to be free of the excess racket.

I thought I'd rescue Debbie from the commotion by engaging her in conversation. Though she is a hearing person, she is fluent in American Sign Language, the language of the deaf, so fluent in fact that many deaf people mistake her for a native signer. One great advantage of American Sign Language—one among many advantages of this beautiful and complex language—is that signers can converse in it in circumstances that would make a spoken conversation impossible. For example, as Carol Padden and Tom Humphries point out in their wonderful book *Deaf in America: Voices from a Culture*, deaf bowlers think nothing of signing their congratulations to a friend who makes a strike three alleys away. Here in the pound, the cacophony all around Debbie and me had no effect on our conversation, and soon we were commenting in detail on the dogs as we passed them.

"I don't have a good feeling about our luck here," I admitted to her.

"Yes, I know. But let's try to imagine these guys outside having a good time. After all, we're seeing them at the worst here. They're probably scared and nervous, not anything like they would be at home."

The dogs looked awful. Either they were barking hysterically or lying flat on the concrete floor, clearly depressed and apathetic. Some of the sad sacks raised their eyes to us as we walked by but lacked the energy to jump up and try to attract our attention like the more manic inmates around them.

Debbie and I moved slowly, trying to imagine each dog in a happier setting, but at the end of the aisle we exchanged discouraged expressions. Then out of the corner of my eye I saw a puppy who seemed different from the rest. He was sitting up, alert and calm, and looking straight at me. In the midst of all the commotion, he seemed intent on making and keeping eye contact, and he was succeeding. This caught my interest as nothing else would have, since eye contact is the lifeblood of communication for deaf people. Everything we take in comes to us through our eyes or skin, and communicating with someone who is not engaging our eyes can be confusing if not impossible. In fact, deaf people in conversation with hearing people are often stymied when the hearing folks break eye contact to look around. When the deaf person looks about and sees nothing, he or she suddenly remembers, "Oh, yes! Hearing people don't *need* to keep consistent visual contact. They glance away just to glance away or glance away because they're distracted by sounds." For a deaf person glancing away means stopping the conversation. And deaf children who "don't want to hear it" don't stuff their fingers in their ears; they scrunch their eyes up tight.

This dog seemed to be ignoring the natural impulse animals have to look away. For most vertebrates maintaining extended eye contact is an aggressive sign, part of a set of behaviors that conveys a challenge to the receiver. But here was this little puppy staring me down, intent on capturing and holding my attention by sheer willpower through the eyes. He wasn't challenging me; that was clear. Rather, he was interested in me, I could tell, but not in a subservient, begging way. There was none of the plea that said, "Won't you please take me home?" in those steady dark eyes, only a frank curiosity and the hint of some fun. "Don't you think we'd like each other?" was how I'd interpret that expression. And perhaps "Don't you think I'm ugly?" but in a self-amused sort of way.

Debbie and I read the tag on the front of the cage. He was half Labrador, half German shepherd, and he had the wriggly long body of a Lab but a scruffy multicolored coat that was 100 percent German shepherd.

"This one," I told Debbie without an instant's hesitation, and she nodded enthusiastically. I was pretty sure she would have tried to argue me out of a choice she considered bad, but I had no doubt that she was dying to get out of there. We both were. Visiting hours at the local jail can make you start to feel locked up too.

At the desk the officials told us that the puppy had been found wandering around in the snow out in the fields near campus. "People dump puppies out there all the time," one man said. "Maybe they think the students will save them. Maybe they don't really care." At any rate, this puppy seemed to be a hardy type. He had survived who knew how many hours or days in the coldest snap Illinois had ever had. I liked the idea of adopting a tough little tyke who could still look out of his cage with that perky interest even after that ordeal in the outdoors.

"I want him," I said.

"Three days," said the clerk.

"Three days?" I asked.

"He's been here four, has to stay seven. If nobody claims him in three more days he's yours."

Outside in the cold I fingerspelled "L-O-X." I was wearing leather gloves that allowed me to make even the minute, subtle finger movements signifying letters without any problem. Native signers use fingerspelling to spell out names and unfamiliar words. Hearing people who know no signing often begin—and frequently end!—by learning the manual alphabet.

Grudgingly, Debbie slipped off her prize mittens, fuzzy red ones a friend had made specially for her, and shoved them in her pocket so she could respond. "What do you mean, 'L-O-X'?" she asked and blew on her hands.

"That's his name. Short for lox, bagels, and cream cheese, my favorite food."

"L-O-X?" She was freezing and slipped the mittens back on her hands.

"Yes, Lox," I told her. Then I added, "If he doesn't work out I can eat him."

Debbie didn't bother slipping off her mittens again. She just looked at me and rolled her eyes.

As the three days passed, I grew increasingly scared that someone would go to the pound and claim Lox, but when I went back there he was. And it was clear he remembered me. I hadn't been mistaken. I'd made as big an impression on this little creature as he had made on me. "About how old do you think he is?" I asked the man behind the counter. I had to ask him to repeat himself a couple of times before I was sure of his answer. "Little do people realize that lipreading a person with a moustache," writes Roy Holcomb in *Silence Is Golden—Sometimes*, "is like hearing half a conversation." Through the thick fuzz overhanging this man's upper lip I finally picked up, "Oh, between two and three months, I reckon." Perfect, I thought. I'd be starting Lox's training from scratch.

Lox couldn't seem to believe his luck as we drove him home from the pound. He kept shoving his nose up under my elbow trying to worm out another affectionate pat or two. And when we got to my apartment he ran around from room to room checking out the floor plan and leaving little puddles wherever he went. Clearly housebreaking was going to be the first order of business—and I mean business.

I had to follow my instincts, since my family hadn't done much training on Happy other than "come!" and "stay!" But as a student minoring in psychology, I was familiar with the theories of behavioral scientists. "All behavior is learned or operant," wrote a behavioral scientist. "Behavior is modified or changed by the events that follow or are contingent upon that behavior." The principles of reinforcing, rewarding, punishing, and modeling the learning theorists had developed all inspired me and merged with my common sense as I set about to train Lox to recognize signed commands. By the time I was through applying classical learning theory, Lox had a working vocabulary of twelve signed commands.

I decided to make the kitchen my command center, so I moved my writing table and all my books right in there where I could be with Lox all day. I covered the floor with newspapers and went back to my dissertation. In this confined space it was easy to keep track of Lox out of the corner of my eye, and every time he started to show signs of having an accident I swooped him up and tossed him outside. By the end of the first day I had figured out how long it took for a meal or a drink to pass through him, so I could pretty much anticipate his needs just by watching the time. I knew that *consistency* was the key word in education—after all I was in training myself to be a teacher. This was going to be a cinch.

Lox soon got the message. Friends and family had complained about that awful weeks-long (sometimes months-long) period between bringing a puppy home and finally accomplishing the housebreaking, but Lox got it down in no time. Twenty-four-hour surveillance, or at least eighteen-hour surveillance, seemed to be the answer. I was cocky about it and bragged to Debbie.

Within two days Lox was scratching at the kitchen door to go out.

Jack, my grumpy housemate in the next apartment, was skeptical but he grudgingly agreed to look after Lox while I went to the library for a few hours. This was to be my first separation from Lox since I had brought him home from the pound, but I was confident about Lox's newly learned skill. I should have worried a bit more, because when I returned home Jack was as mad as hell. "He shit here, he peed there. . . ." The guy was so furious he was sputtering, and finally he just dragged me through the house to see the evidence for myself. Meanwhile, Lox was so excited to see me he was giving the place another once-over sprinkle. My housemate took the idea of eye contact one step too far, I thought. He leaned in close to my face and said, "Get the filthy mutt out of my place and don't let me see him again."

Back in my apartment, Lox almost immediately scratched on the kitchen door to go out. It took a few more accidents at various people's houses to see that for Lox the *house* in *housebroken* meant our house only. Everywhere else, including other apartments, was the big outside world for Lox.

Next I tackled "come!" I tied a rope to Lox's collar, and every time I signed "come!" I pulled the rope to me. After a few attempts Lox got the hang of it and I could reward his good work handsomely with pieces of cheese or raw beef. Soon he knew the rule fairly well. Then if he did not respond properly I would pull the rope a little to give him the clue that he was supposed to come to see me. During the day I would work on the command at unpredictable moments, and after a few days Lox had mastered "come!"

"Stay!" was next. I'd make sure Lox was sitting and

then signal "stay!" by holding my palm down stiffly. If
he moved or walked away, I would jerk him back to his
place and start over. In the beginning if he stayed where
I asked him to, I would sign "okay"—a relaxed wave—
meaning "You're released," and then would reward
him. Lox would watch carefully for "okay," and this
turned out to be a good way to increase his attention
span and visual concentration.

Once Lox had mastered "stay!" I would scratch my
head or pick up a pencil, magazine, or newspaper,
tempting him with false signs. At first he'd get up and
I would jerk him back to his position. Slowly, though,
he learned to discriminate "okay" from other
handshapes or movements.

I started fingerspelling the word "walk" to Lox right
away, and he was soon able to comprehend the minute
finger movements as a sign that we were going out. I'd
tease him sometimes by changing around the spelling or
spelling other words, and at first he'd jump up in excitement at anything. But I'd signal "no" and he would
sit down, all alertness, waiting for the right spelling. Finally he'd get it and off we'd go. My friends found it
hard to believe that Lox could read fingerspelling, and
we had to demonstrate many times to prove it wasn't a
trick.

I also taught Lox to bark on command, though at first
I wasn't sure how to proceed. During our roughhousing,
when he would bark in playful excitement, I'd make the
sign for "bark," linking it in his mind with the act. Then
I'd coach him with the sign again and again in our
training sessions. I'd alternate between that sign and another gesture, cupping my ear as if I couldn't hear him.
Soon every time I cupped my ear or signed "bark!" he
would bark nonstop until I put my hand down.

Once Lox could bark on command, I set about linking the commands "come!" and "bark!" with the ringing of the doorbell—the goal was for Lox to signal every time somebody rang the bell so I wouldn't have to rely on a light signal. I enlisted friends to help me by ringing the bell, and between my teaching and Lox's natural instinct to protect me, the connection was made. Since I was making things up as I went along, I couldn't figure out how to teach Lox to come up and paw me to signal that the doorbell was ringing, but I could feel the vibrations of his wild barking, so his signaling worked all right. One thing, though—Lox seemed supremely uninterested in or oblivious to the ringing of the phone, and I never succeeded in teaching him to signal that someone was trying to reach me that way.

Two weeks after I brought Lox home he became very, very ill. The vet looked grim as he delivered the one-word diagnosis: "Distemper." Lox had picked up this common canine disease at the pound, and the vet went on to explain that only 5 percent of dogs contracting it survived. The vet offered to put Lox to sleep—and he had to make the awful suggestion several times, since I think I didn't *want* to understand him. When I finally interpreted his suggestion, I firmly refused. But often during this period, as Lox grew sicker and sicker, I was to ask myself if I'd made the right decision.

All his spontaneous puppy qualities disappeared. I moved my writing table back into the living room so Lox could lie on the couch and watch me write. I knew he was comforted by my presence, and he always at least tried to show an interest in the chicken soup I offered him by spoon. Finally, though, his appetite was almost completely gone and Debbie started trying to interest me in looking for another puppy, hoping to ease the loss that seemed inevitable. I even scanned the ads she shoved in front of me, but it made me feel guilty to think about getting another dog when Lox was lying there dying. Nursing Lox, spoon-feeding him that way, and carrying him outside periodically only made our bond grow stronger just when I suppose I should have been trying to let go.

Through it all he kept his characteristic directness. He was always looking me in the eye. By the second week of his illness he was completely couchridden, and at night I carried him to my bed so he could sleep next to me. It was a long four weeks, but one morning I awoke to find Lox on his feet on the bed sniffing and licking me and waiting for me to lock eyes with him. He was almost completely recovered, in the same way a very sick baby often snaps back into wholesome good health overnight. From that day on he was slurping up all the chicken soup I could spoon into him and then bouncing around for more. By six weeks after he had fallen ill he was back to his old self again—and our friendship was cemented forever.

I loved him not only for being himself but for pulling through against all odds, and he seemed to understand that I had done all I could to help him recover, even if toward the end that meant merely keeping him company. The bond we had was something special—much more profound than anything I'd experienced with any other dog—and his loyalty to me was almost *too* intense. He hated being separated from me and he got very protective when visitors came. As he grew, his powerful bark scared lots of people away, but it gave me a sense of security. I could be deep in concentration at my desk when the very feel of his barking would suddenly alert me that there was someone approaching the door.

One version of a famous folk story from deaf culture has it that the great French educator, the Abbé de l'Epée, who helped establish a school system for the deaf in his country, began his career when he knocked on the door of a country cottage, received no answer, and finally entered to sit quietly by as two deaf sisters sewed by the fire, completely unaware that he was there. Besides dramatizing the moment in which the Abbé's vocation crystallized for him, that story also illustrates the deaf person's vulnerability to being approached unaware. Most deaf people have flashing lights connected to their doorbells to alert them to a visitor, but unless they feel the footsteps on the stairs, there's nothing to alert them to someone's approach *before* the doorlight flashes. And lights do no good when you're fast asleep. Even worse, bulbs burn out. Sometimes a person doesn't realize that nobody's been by in quite a long while. With Lox, all these problems disappeared from my life. I was left with only the problem of soothing desirable visitors after Lox had scared them out of their wits.

In his smooth adaptation to deafness and its modes of communication, Lox was following in a family tradition I had always relied on. My parents and two hearing brothers, Dunbar and David, learned a lot about how the world in general views deafness—as a near-tragic medical disaster that permanently shuts its "victims" out of normal (read "hearing") society—from the experiences of my older deaf brother, Jonathan. When I was born deaf, they vowed that I would grow up with as much access to the treasures and pleasures of society as they themselves had. They meant to see to it that I had the means to be proud of who I was, not special because I was deaf, but special because I was myself.

Unlike many families of deaf children who never

quite master alternative ways of communicating, my parents and brothers went to extremes to make certain I was included in every minute of family life and that every piece of information, every thought, joke, insult, or bit of nonsense, was communicated to me. Since I had no hearing whatsoever, they realized they would have to address my eyes, not my ears, and they were constantly seeking ways of making language visible. They were not exposed to sign language, but they used their imagination and intelligence in communicating. They made certain they were easy to lipread, they tended to overgesture, they used their hands and miming skills freely, and very early—far earlier than is usual—they began to teach me to recognize written words.

Research shows that when they enter school most deaf children lack a wide and diverse range of early childhood experiences and especially of language, whether English or American Sign Language. Thus they have trouble reading and writing and this often leads to learning difficulties and delayed progress in school. But my family immersed me in books and ideas. They placed a high value on education, and everyone, including myself, was expected to finish graduate school and become a professional. My parents and brothers gave me lots of encouragement and tutoring during my early years and they made sure to invite accomplished and successful deaf adults into our home to serve as role models. Again, this was in direct contrast to general practice until the late 1970s, since many families—and schools too!—tended to keep deaf adults and others from the deaf community out of their deaf children's lives in the vain attempt to make their children "normal." To my way of thinking, they only succeeded in reinforcing a sense of differentness, and sometimes a deep loneliness. But thanks to the efforts and sensitivity of my family, I never once considered myself "abnormal" and never doubted that I would attain my doctorate and become a professor. My goal, now achieved, was to become a professor of deaf education, teaching teachers of the deaf.

I trained Lox to stay close to me when we went out and to respond to "okay," which meant he was free to roam around. I am convinced that the companionable and finely trained Avalanche served as a role model for Lox and eased his training. Still, I spent many, many evenings working on the "stay!" command with Lox. I took him to the area of the campus known as the Quad and left him to wait for me, first for minutes, then for hours. Eventually, after much spying and jumping out of hiding on my part, Lox would wait for me anywhere, and my sense of satisfaction and security at that was immeasurable.

Several months after getting Lox, my search for my first postdoctorate job began and I had to travel to California for some interviews. I asked a friend who lived on a farm to care for Lox, but within days he had had it. Lox may have been responsive to me, but according to this fellow he was a complete pain to take care of, so the fellow motored Lox into town and dropped him with Jack, my grumpy across-the-hall neighbor. Jack had had enough of Lox on first meeting and only wanted to do the minimum now: he left Lox in the backyard all day and shoved him into my empty apartment during the night. Well, it might have been loneliness and it might have been out-and-out rebellion, but Lox spent that stretch of nights tearing up the apartment, and when I finally reached home I opened the door to a kind of furniture stew. The place looked like a cook had chopped the contents and stirred them up with a huge wooden spoon—and then dusted the whole simmering mess with feathers (my treasured sleeping bag, which had gone to so many countries of the world!) and paper (my thesis looked as if the government had ordered it shredded).

When I stomped across the hall to ask Jack if he knew what had been going on, I roused a pair of crossed arms and a narrow, shifting gaze. "Talk to Lox about it, not me," was the nonverbal message in that angry stance. "I'm not your baby-sitter, dog-sitter, or house-sitter." I guess he thought I got what I deserved for bringing Lox into our quiet house.

Everyone I knew on campus loved the story of the shredded thesis. It reminded the students of the times they'd asked for extensions on papers because "the dog ate my first draft." And my advisor loved it because for once the story was true. It followed me everywhere, and even the librarian, in that hushed, serious temple of study, asked me how the dog had enjoyed my thesis. "Did he find it a little too dry?" she ventured to ask. I hated disappointing all those who loved the story by telling them I had another copy, fully bound, safe on an upper shelf.

I took frequent trips to California after that, since my family and Anne, who had accepted my marriage proposal, lived there and it seemed the right place for us to settle. But on my next trip back I took Lox, and he went happily and untranquilized into the kennel the airline provided. It moved me to see how willingly he entered this confined space, and I watched the little cage bounce away from me on the conveyor belt with some sense of guilt. The bond between me and Lox was so tight that he trusted me completely, even when I guided him into new, uncomfortable situations.

In this case, I might have wished he'd exhibited a little of the wild rebelliousness he'd shown to Jack, because the airline mistakenly routed poor Lox to Texas and Colorado before finally setting him back on course to California. It was twelve hours before we met up again—and twelve hours before he'd had a chance to relieve himself. At the baggage claim, where Anne and I had been waiting for half a day, Lox shot out of the kennel, showing his joy at seeing me—but only in passing, as he headed straight through the crowd to the airport door.

Anne had never cared much for dogs, but she hit it off with Lox immediately, and for the same reason I had. It was that fabulous, unwavering eye contact. Anne is deaf, but because of her extensive auditory training during her formative years, she is able to function as hard of hearing*—that is, able to hear some sounds with the help of amplification. For some reason I was never able to benefit much from hearing aids. You have to have a gift for it—like natural piano players do for the keyboard—but I never did. Anne is one of those gifted people. Still, like all hard of hearing and deaf people, she depends on her eyes for communication as heavily as hearing people depend on their ears. When she saw that Lox too was a "visual type," she instantly accepted my constant companion as her own as well.

I took a job in Visalia, California, working at College of the Sequoias as the coordinator of the hearing im-

*The broad term *hard of hearing* covers all levels of hearing loss from mild to serious. The lighter the loss, the greater the auditory discrimination and the smaller the distortion. Hearing aids can compensate for hearing loss to some degree but they do not perfect hearing the way glasses correct distorted vision.

paired program there, and some time later Anne and I were married in a small, lovely ceremony on the beach in Santa Barbara. We lived together with Lox in a house without a fence in Visalia, and struggled with the terrible heat that wilted the people (but not the crops) of the San Joaquin Valley every summer. Lox had his own way of cooling off—by jumping uninvited into various backyard swimming pools. Finally I had to have a fence built, but this did nothing to keep him inside—he dug under every day—until we came up with the notion of keeping him busy with huge beef bones the butcher would save for us. He would spend hours, *days*, on a single bone, completely forgetting about roaming and swimming until he had gnawed it to his satisfaction and then buried it. As long as we could get him a new bone on the day he buried the old one, Lox stayed home. It wasn't until we did some landscaping two years later that we realized how many bones he had buried. Our friend who did the rototilling thought for one horrific minute that he had discovered the scene of a grisly mass murder—not unheard of in California.

Anne's father, too, fell in love with Lox. He admitted to me that Lox was the first dog he had ever liked, and then went on to tell me something I hadn't known about the relationship between Lox and me. "You know, that dog talks to you all the time. As a matter of fact, I get the feeling that dog has the gift of gab!"

"What do you mean?" I asked him.

"Why, now, take a look at this. Every time he looks straight at you he's making sounds galore that you'd swear was his part of a very animated conversation. He's singing and squealing and growling and just edging up on barking to you while you're talking or signing to him!"

I had had no idea Lox was vocalizing to me, but I really enjoyed the notion. I talked to Lox a lot myself, though I had taught him a series of manual commands, or hand signals. I wouldn't dream of saying I actually taught Lox sign language; that would be like saying a dog knows English, when he or she is actually responding to specific words rather than the whole complex web of meaning and rules. But he did know and respond perfectly to twelve manual commands: "come," "go back," "don't," "near me," "sit," "go to bed," "jump," "wait," "stay," "go after it," "let's go," and "okay."

But even beyond that, Lox responded to the environment in a way that allowed me and Anne to relax our visual vigilance a little. Hearing people are often surprised to learn how effective and thorough our vision and sense of touch are in keeping deaf people well-informed about the environment. (In fact, most deaf people believe that if it weren't for hearing people, "the others," and *their* reliance on hearing, we'd never even notice the lack of auditory stimuli.) Still, vision is limited by walls, eyelids, deep concentration on one object (such as a book or television screen), and sometimes pillows over the eyes, so it's not unusual for deaf people to be surprised suddenly by changes in the environment—for instance, people suddenly appearing, disappearing, or trying to get our attention through a barrier to vision; phones ringing; timers going off; toast popping; kettles boiling; and so on. It's just this sort of information Lox learned to bring us. Every time someone rang the doorbell or knocked at the door, he would come up to me to make some kind of eye contact and then run toward the door barking. But there were other, less predictable instances in which he was truly a lifesaver.

One cold evening in January, Anne and I were enjoying the fire in our fireplace, having a sort of pajama party and feeling cozy and snug. Without my knowing it, Anne went off to the garage to get some more firewood, which we kept inside the garage out of the rain. Somehow she got herself locked inside the garage. All the escapes were blocked: the garage door itself was locked on the outside with a padlock, the window was stuck tight, the door to the house had locked behind her—and it was *freezing* out there. She pulled her pajamas tight around her and pounded vigorously on the door.

In response to the pounding, Lox came to me and simply locked eyes with me. Because there was no visitor at the door, he didn't bark—he just caught me with his intense gaze and wouldn't let it go. It took me a while to notice, what with my dreamy gazing into the fire, but when I finally glanced his way he took off and then came back to me, signaling for me to follow. By the time I found Anne, she was turning blue with the cold and imagining any number of ghastly things. After all, if a locked door could slam between her and the house, one could accidentally close between Lox and me . . . and I could have fallen asleep in front of the fire, and then, and then, and then. . . .

"Lox, the Great," we often called him after that. The idea of having him for breakfast never crossed my mind.

Lox became quite a celebrity in Visalia. For one thing, he was a highly *visible* personality, because I had trained him to wait for me on top of my car to keep him away from other dogs. But more than that, reporters in Central California were fascinated by his work as a nonprofessional signal dog.* Though deaf people had probably been training dogs to work for them since dogs and humans found mutual benefits in each other's company, professionally trained signal dogs were just becoming publicized. Although deaf people had always found ways to train their dogs, in the late 1960s and early 1970s a surge of public interest prompted the establishment of many signal dog programs and a spate of publicity. By the time we moved to Fresno in 1979, where I was to teach at the university, many people had met Lox's piercing gaze coming at them from their morning newspaper over breakfast. He was a popular dog and a wonderful conversation piece—people who feared deafness or misunderstood it (a great many people fall into these categories) and who would never have risked starting a conversation with me if they knew I was deaf stopped when they recognized Lox on the street and found themselves asking questions before they even remembered their nervousness. I was to learn and relearn one of the greatest unsung blessings of owning a dog: it gets people together who would never have chatted with each other, whether it be standing on a street corner or at a formal conference or a lecture. I'd certainly recommend walking dogs over ads or dating agencies to the single person intent on meeting folks of the opposite sex.

* * *

*Although the term *hearing dogs* was the one that reporters used originally, people in the deaf community and the instructors of working dogs prefer *signal dogs*. This preference rests on the fact that the dogs don't really hear for us but rather signal, or alert, us to acoustic signals. Where *hearing dog* seemed to raise the public's expectations about what the dogs could do, *signal dog* reinforces the accurate image of independent deaf people making use of a convenient signaling device.

It was another cold evening just before Christmas, and I was luxuriating in my new leisure time. I had just turned in my students' final grades and Anne and I were quietly celebrating the end of the semester in front of the fire. We had our sleeping bags there and talked about our Christmas plans until we nearly drifted off to sleep. During the evening Lox had seemed restless and had needed to go out often. Now he lay beside us very quietly—too quietly, we thought, since Lox was less a cuddler than a somewhat macho protector. But we welcomed his unusual wish to relax very close to us, and we all fell asleep with the fire dying out on its own.

In the morning, Lox was still asleep in the corner of the family room. He tended to be lazy in the morning, spending a long time "in bed," but this time the very stillness of his head when I called his name gave me a premonition, and in a stride or two I was by his side, realizing the worst: my dear friend Lox, only eight years old, was dead.

I shook Anne out of her sleep. With that, I crawled over and started to pet Lox again and again. Anne knelt by him and hugged him. Touching him over and over, we yearned to wake him out of his "sleep." With my hand on his shoulder and on his hip, I could almost feel those familiar muscles move. I so wanted them to move. There! But no. No tiny flexing or twitching beneath the skin. No little ripple of a muscle that would be followed by a great, lazy morning stretch and a yawn. Lox's body was stiff. It was lifeless.

We cried very hard and were very helpless, paralyzed. Then we felt the need to share our grief with our friends. Anne called our close friends Alta and Lee and they came over immediately. They were also very fond of Lox. They held us and cried with us. Suddenly we started to sense an emptiness everywhere in the house.

Out of the corner of my eye I would catch a glimpse of Lox, coming in where he always came in. I would turn, but he wasn't there. Emptiness. And there grew an emptiness in me, in Anne and me.

After crying for about an hour and talking about him and how young he was, we decided it was important to get an autopsy. We called the office of our vet, Roger, but because it was Saturday, he was off and we were referred to another vet on duty. He offered his services. We refused and insisted that we be in touch with Roger. A few minutes later Roger called and agreed to meet us immediately. Dr. Roger Tsuruda was not just a vet but a special friend to Lox, too. At that moment we needed him not just as a technically skilled person but as a friend.

Lox's death—from acute pancreatitis—hit Anne and me very hard. After the autopsy Lox was cremated, and we went out and buried him in the Sierra foothills. It was appropriate and fitting for him to be part of nature again, and where in nature he found peace Anne and I were seeking healing. We had never been without him as a married couple. We had been a tight family unit, and had never given a moment's thought to losing him. Now we had to go through the classic stages of grieving to incorporate and accept our loss.

Slowly, slowly, the guilty thoughts ("Could we have helped?" "In all our end-of-semester and Christmas busyness, did we miss his signals that he was in trouble?"), the sudden flashes of denial ("But wasn't that Lox running with that little terrier?"), and the disappointments accompanying the new realization of our loss began to recede as we came to accept the fact that Lox was gone. Still, that empty place in our household never closed up and we were aware all the time of the missing presence. Some friends found it peculiar. "After all, he was just a dog," said a few, who didn't mean to be insensitive but simply couldn't fathom how our private life had changed. Others, though, saw the significance of our losing Lox and their sympathy eased us through. And when Debbie wrote a long letter reminding me of how different, and perhaps how very abbreviated, Lox's life would have been had I not rescued him from the pound, I felt the crisis of our grief passing.

But yet we found ourselves on edge a lot, with anxiety tightening our breathing a lot more than it ever had before in our married life. In fact, that first night in our own house without Lox had been a little like toughing it out in a haunted house—not knowing who, or *what*, would show up and when. The house seemed very big suddenly, and both of us confessed in the morning to thinking about the rooms behind the rooms behind the room that we slept in. Was there anything going on in the depths of the house that we should have known about? I think that night we realized how completely we had depended not only on our eyes but on Lox's ears. His vigilance was our safety measure and without it our sleep was very fitful indeed.

After a week we decided to borrow a good friend's dog, thinking that maybe we could regain our sense of security and cure our insomnia. But the dog, Trixie, couldn't stand me, and every time we met he would bark at me as if I were a total stranger. No matter how many times I came home from work, no matter how often I got up for a drink of water in the night, Trixie would go nuts at the sight of me. In fact he was lots more relaxed and easy to calm down when *real* strangers came to the house! This was certainly no solution.

We were really in a state, not only of anxiety but of superalertness as well. It wasn't until after his death that we discovered how much Lox had really done for our peace of mind. Now the phone would ring, the doorbell would buzz, strangers and friends would knock on the front or back door, people would wander through our front yard, cats would shoot into our backyard and begin to fight, the smoke alarm would go off in response to burning food in the frying pan, and visitors would actually open the door and peer around it, then venture into the house and surprise us in our underwear! We discovered that what we thought was a calm, peaceful home was really an absolute hive of activity and surprises. And Lox had taken it all in stride. "Oh, I hope he didn't feel unappreciated!" Anne said to me. I had to admit that maybe he *was* just a little, if not *un*appreciated, then *under*appreciated. We had come to rely on him for so long we hadn't even realized how well he did his job.

We had to set up an electrical light system to alert us to phone calls on the TDD (telephone device for the deaf) and to the ringing of the front doorbell. But the Fresno house was big—four bedrooms, a large living room, a family room, and three bathrooms—so it was impossible to install a light in every room. We ended up missing important calls, visitors, and deliveries— thereby discovering *another* thing Lox had done for us. Not only had he kept our anxiety level down, but he had also kept our irritability in check as well. Now we had potential misses all the time, and whenever that happened the irritability level soared well into the "furious" range.

Over the weeks other clues to Lox's importance surfaced. For example, our next-door neighbor came over to let us know he'd been burglarized. Someone had broken into the house and hauled out many of his valuables. When we told him that Lox was gone, he realized that he too had been depending on Lox's vigorous barking to alert him to possible trouble. And in the course of time it became clear that five nearby households had depended on Lox's skills as a watchdog—they all missed him now and paid their condolences.

Lox's absence was perhaps most inconvenient when we went out camping. Anne and I loved to go off into the woods, sleeping either in a tent or in our well-equipped pickup truck. But the first time we went camping without Lox we were nervous about intruders and emergencies as we had never been before.

I kept thinking we'd get used to that feeling, and finally fell asleep. In the morning I was ready for adventure, but poor Anne slept in until twelve. All night she had lain awake with her imagination running wild—in her mind's eye she saw bears, wolves, strange unidentifiable beasts, and human homicidal maniacs crackling and stomping up to our pickup and then crashing unexpectedly inside, so she didn't fall asleep until the first light of morning appeared.

On the second night we tied a rope to the inside handle of the door to our pickup truck and then to a bundle of junk. The idea was that if someone opened the door, we would be jerked awake. I suppose it wasn't a bad plan, but after two nights we came home early, our camping trip ruined by paranoia and wild imaginings.

That dog! He had not only kept us worry-free, he had even kept us in shape! Every day Lox had quite aggressively reminded me that he needed some exercise, and both Anne and I took him out for long walks in the country, which opened up a block from our house. It was wonderful to stroll through the pasturelands and along the rows of grapes, cotton, corn, fruit trees, and nut trees. This was a level of our life that we valued highly and enjoyed fully, but with Lox gone we became lazy. It's true we went out for walks, often joined by our dear friends and neighbors Lee and Alta, but Anne now refused to go out at night, and I missed the fabulous dark open sky and the starry country sky. I admit that without Anne and Lox beside me those nighttime strolls took on a slightly risky reel and I found myself sitting by the fire in the evenings more than I ever had.

This was ridiculous! We were going all nervous and soft. We had to get another dog.

We started with a list Anne sent away for after reading an article on signal dogs for the deaf,* and we chose Canine Companions for Independence, in Santa Rosa, California, as the most potentially interesting. What distinguished CCI from others we read about was the two-week "boot camp" it offered as part of its program for people receiving signal dogs. The idea of training the owners as well as the dogs appealed to us, considering how much Lox had taught us—if belatedly—about how he could participate in our lives.

We called CCI for an appointment, and two weeks later drove the two hundred or so miles northward to have a look. CCI trains dogs to match to people with all sorts of needs; our interviewer, Kerry Knaus, had her own wheelchair dog, Abdul, who demonstrated more about how useful a well-trained dog could be than any amount of conversation would have done. Abdul handled such complex tasks as picking up things from the floor for Kerry and pulling her wheelchair through trouble spots such as muddy or sandy ground, up steep slopes, and so on. Since pay phones tend to be too high

*For a complete list, write to the Hearing Dog Resource Center, P.O. Box 1080, Renton, WA 98057-1080, or call 800-869-6898 (voice/TDD). To date, at least twenty-five different schools for training signal dogs exist in the United States (not including private individuals who train dogs for deaf people).

for people in wheelchairs to reach, Abdul would take down the receiver for Kerry, who would then use a stick to press the buttons. And Abdul would even turn light switches on and off for her!

Well, I was very impressed with what I saw at CCI and the interview, but I wanted to make absolutely sure that there had been no report of animal abuse or incidents of possible cruelty at CCI. It would be nice to have one or two issues in *Consumer Reports* on dog programs. I called the Better Business Bureau in Santa Rosa to find out if anyone had filed reports against CCI; I got some information to contact the Public Prosecution Office in Santa Rosa. I did and spoke with several persons. Much to my relief, there was nothing filed in their offices against CCI. And much to my joy, one person referred me to a court reporter and clerk who was very knowledgeable about the program. She went into detail about how wonderful the program was and especially about their respect for animals. The staff members at CCI know how happy dogs are to be working if paired with the right persons. That is a fundamental principle with them. It warmed my heart to hear that they had a philosophy I knew to be vital. I knew Lox was happy when he was kept busy and treated as my sidekick rather than as a pampered pet.

We were convinced that a professionally trained working dog matched our needs precisely and initiated the paperwork that would put us on CCI's waiting list. If we were accepted into the program, we would have our dog in about six months. But when we started doing the paperwork we wondered if there had perhaps been some misunderstanding—did they think we wanted to adopt a child? The forms, the letters of recommendation required, the questionnaires regarding our personalities and emotional profiles—these folks were serious! They wanted to know exactly what kind of people we were, what kind of life we led, and how we would interact with one of their graduates—a dog with a serious commitment to her career.

One of CCI's objectives in attempting to elicit detailed self-descriptions was to determine what difficult situations the applicants were likely to encounter, what dogs they would be well matched with, and what breeds it would be best to avoid. It was also important to determine whether the applicants would be able to tolerate the public's widespread ignorance about working dogs and the laws that pertained to them. Working dogs are legally permitted to accompany their owners everywhere, even places where nonworking dogs are not allowed. Owners of working dogs often become one- or two-person institutions of learning, sometimes merely pointing out the law, sometimes having to insist upon it—as we were soon to learn.

A month after our grueling bout of paperwork, we learned that we had been accepted into the program and would receive a dog from CCI. Our two-week training in Santa Rosa would take place six months hence. Like prospective adopters awaiting that phone call that would make them instant parents, our imaginations were completely taken up with what our dog might be like. We stared at all puppies we passed on the street, constantly had to stop each other from impulsively buying or accepting a free offer of the absolute "perfect" dog to fill Lox's place, and hoped we'd done the right thing by choosing CCI. Had we represented ourselves accurately enough? Would they make the right choice for us? It was a long six months and we still missed Lox, but in his characteristically direct way he had propelled us on to our next exciting and wonderfully enriching dog adventure.

CHAPTER 2

Falling in Love

NORTHERN California in August. It was dry and *hot*, and Anne and I were on the road headed from one California hot spot, Fresno, to another—Santa Rosa, in the heart of the Sonoma Wine Country. We drove through the landscape known locally as "California blonde"— gentle yellow rolling hills dotted with clumps of oak— feeling as if we were finally headed off on a camping trip again. In a way we were, since for the next two weeks we would be sleeping in a tent in our niece's backyard. But this was to be no ordinary camping trip. CCI had summoned us to a training session, where we would meet and get to know our signal dog.

It had been a long wait, and we were very excited. Anne and I tried to keep each other focused on the serious nature of the trip. CCI's introductory mailer outlining training course policies and procedures read:

> The CCI training course lasts two weeks. However, an additional time period may be required for those individuals who have unique or additional training needs.

Two weeks! How much could there be to learn for a dog lover like me, especially one who had already trained a dog to meet his particular needs? Well, I thought, I can look forward to the time as a well-needed vacation, a time to relax, see some sights, maybe go on some wine tastings and some day trips to the ocean.

A very serious warning ended the CCI mailer:

A participant who at any time during training . . . fails to handle a canine placement according to CCI requirements . . . may be deemed ineligible for participation in the program.

I never gave it a second thought. After all, I'd had dogs all my life. How different could the CCI requirements be from what intuition and experience had taught me about getting along with dogs?

Yes, we rolled along quite merrily in the hundred-degree-plus heat, never realizing we were heading for two weeks' worth of the longest, most difficult, and most exciting and satisfying days of our lives. All we could think about was that we would finally be meeting the dog we had waited for so impatiently for six months. What we didn't realize then, at least not fully, was that I myself—and Anne through me—was about to be taught to function as a team with a professionally trained working dog who had been acquiring her expertise over the preceding two years. It was a question of expert meets novice—and I was the novice.

Santa Rosa is a pretty little city characterized by lovely old-fashioned houses and a distinctive hometown flavor. Our niece, along with some college companions, had rented one of these houses for the summer, and we gratefully let them welcome us after our 250-mile drive. Then we pitched our tent and set up our Coleman stove for our stint of backyard camping. Since all CCI training session participants are asked to make their own living arrangements, this setup couldn't have been more perfect for us. Aside from those last nervous trips after Lox died, we hadn't been camping in ages, and both Anne and I sorely missed it. But here, with our backs to the house and with the open fields spreading out all around us, we felt that peaceful sense of sinking into nature and remembering our part in it all.

Both of us had been terribly busy over the last six months, I at the university and Anne in her job as a registered nurse at the hospital. As we laid out our sleeping bags, we luxuriated in the feeling that our hectic schedules were behind us for a while.

That night CCI did nothing to disabuse us of our holiday feeling—quite the opposite. The staff put on a full-blown banquet for our group to launch the new training session for us and allow us to meet our fellow trainees.

It was a great way to start—we could do a lot of people-watching, the way you do at a party, and get to know our tablemates one by one gradually over the evening. Besides the instructors and boot camp leaders, there were fourteen trainees. Three of us were deaf— Anne and I, who were counted as one since we were getting a dog together, Scott Jackson, a college student, and Denise, a fortyish housewife and mother.

Like deaf people everywhere, we "deafies" gravitated to each other and began our acquaintance by discussing how thrilled we were to find that the staff had provided an interpreter for us during the banquet. An interpreter is a professionally trained go-between in a conversation between a deaf and a hearing person who signs the hearing person's remarks to the deaf person and repeats the deaf person's signed or spoken remarks (if the deaf person's speech is difficult for hearing people to understand) to the hearing person. Trained interpreters are under oath to adhere to rigid standards, which include interpreting *everything* that is said, in the tone in which it is expressed, and interjecting nothing. It was one thing to provide an interpreter for the training, but it indicated a deeper level of sensitivity to provide one at a social event. Things can get pretty wild for deaf people at parties, where conversations often begin and end simultaneously all around them. If you're depending on your eyes to tell you who's going to speak next, and there are even only five or six people around you all talking at once (at the banquet there were three times that many), you might have to be moving pretty fast to keep up. We all agreed that the presence of the interpreter boded well for the training. Thinking about the many faculty parties I'd attended, with all my powers of concentration focused on guessing who might speak next, I suddenly felt absolutely delighted to be in this type of social situation, and I could tell my companions felt similarly pleased with the hospitality.

CCI's director and founder, Bonnie Bergin, gave us a little background on CCI, and over the course of our stay there we would learn the story of how a sudden brilliant vision became a reality. Bonnie and her husband, fresh out of college, wanted a little adventure and took off globe-trotting. During their travels in the Middle East, they saw people everywhere with deformed or missing limbs, missing eyes, and other kinds of serious disabilities. Most of these people were terribly poor and had no assistance of any kind. It is not easy for some Americans to imagine disabled people with no access to the canes, crutches, wheelchairs, prostheses, braces, guide dogs, and other essential support devices they need, but millions of disabled people around the world never have a prayer of receiving this help.

Bonnie often recounted one incident that remained vivid in her mind. Looking from the balcony of a rooftop restaurant in Ankara, Turkey, during lunch, she saw a quadriplegic man using his shoulders, arms, elbows, and wrists to drag his body slowly but persistently across the six-lane highway below. Stunned, Bonnie glanced behind her at the Turkish diners and was doubly shocked to realize that even those who saw him glanced away, indifferent. This was the norm in Ankara—nothing to get concerned about.

Although this was perhaps Bonnie's most dramatic experience it was only one of many similar sights. Still, some people found makeshift ways of doing things, and Bonnie began to notice disabled people using donkeys and burros to aid them in the agonizingly difficult work of survival.

Memories of Bonnie's trip haunted her after she returned to the United States and entered Sonoma State University in Northern California to get her master's degree in special education. She was particularly revisited by images of the donkeys in their service to the disabled. This was a time, in the early 1970's, when ideas about disabilities were changing in our own country— new attitudes and programs were bringing disabled people out of the institutions where they had been hidden away and into the mainstream of society. What was it about the donkeys that drew Bonnie's attention in this context? And then, pow, the idea of service dogs struck her. American society would never accept donkeys, but dogs could do the job of aiding those with special needs and they would find acceptance here.

People in the dog world rejected the idea out of hand. How could disabled people with limited strength and stamina accomplish what they needed to accomplish— involving as it did so much lifting, pushing, pulling, jerking, and shaking—with their dogs? Ridiculous!

Bonnie was undaunted. She combined everything she knew about psychology and came up with an approach not only to training dogs but to educating the disabled on how to use and control them. She began to find support for her idea and create the beginnings of a training center in Santa Rosa, California, and simultaneously she developed an instructors' training program that set the tone for the boot camp experience. Any potential dog recipient would have to learn how—and be willing—to get inside the dog's mind and know how it thinks, feels, sees, and wants. That person would have to be able to understand how the dog perceives the environment, what it expects from people in general but especially the master, why it will respond effectively—and when and why it will not.

That approach, combined with a unique and equally stringent program of training for the dogs themselves, formed the philosophical basis for the CCI adventure. After years of effort the institute was a going concern and there were now four categories of canine companions available at CCI—service dogs (serving people with body movement and strength impairments), signal dogs (serving the deaf), social dogs (for people who are housebound or otherwise isolated), and specialty dogs (for people with multiple disabilities and/or who are elderly and increasingly dependent)—at five regional centers across the country.* All these, as Bonnie explained, are made available to specially selected applicants with a great range of unique needs.

Bonnie emphasized the phrase *specially selected*. A great deal of effort goes into choosing applicants who will make the most of their dogs, and as much effort again goes into making the perfect match between human and dog. Inevitably, though, mismatches occur, and we would learn that there are three classic categories of matches that fail to work. The first involves applicants

*Bonnie has also helped to organize similar centers abroad, particularly in Israel, Canada, Holland, and France.

who think they are seeking a means of achieving more independence but are actually so accustomed to being dependent on others that they are unable or unwilling to reshape their lives. Once the novelty of owning a dog wears off, these applicants slide back into reliance on others and the dog becomes increasingly unresponsive. In the few inevitable cases where such mismatches survive boot camp, the dog is recalled to CCI and the relationship is terminated.

In the second classic mismatch, the applicant proves to have difficulty assuming control over the dog. He or she seems to want to view the dog as a mechanical push-button device rather than a living entity that needs, and seeks, strong leadership. This applicant has no will for giving orders and is unable to direct the dog with the necessary assertiveness and lack of ambiguity. The instructors are on the lookout for lapses in leadership throughout boot camp, and applicants who cannot muster adequate authority leave without a dog.

The third classic problem is somewhat subtle and hard to detect during training. One might call it a case of personality conflict—the applicant simply doesn't take to the dog, or vice versa. As in any long-term relationship, the chemistry has to be there or it doesn't work. The instructors are constantly watching for the smallest hints and intuitions regarding the bonding, or lack thereof, between humans and the dogs they are matched with. Bonnie admitted to us that in a few cases no dogs could be found to please certain people, and she suspected that there would be no dogs anywhere in the world that would do the trick for some of these folks.

There were fifteen in our group, and in fact one person would prove unable to exert control and would leave CCI without a dog. Although we were all hopeful, eager, and terribly curious about the matches the instructors had made for us, we would not meet the dogs until the training formally began. This night was the time to get to know our fellow classmates.

We were an assortment. Under most circumstances I would never dream of identifying a group of people in terms of their disabilities, but in this case such a roll call testifies to the wide applicability of Bonnie's idea. Grouped around our banquet table that first night in addition to Anne and me were the following participants:

- Seven-year-old Jennifer, crippled by a rare childhood disease that prevented the normal development of her spinal cord, used an electric mobility-designed wheelchair.
- Catherine, in her early thirties, had juvenile arthritis. She walked with a cane, was visually impaired, and had had to give up her successful practice as a speech therapist owing to her disease.
- Jessie, who had become a paraplegic as a result of a car accident, was in her early twenties and was studying to become a special education teacher.
- Douglas, a quadriplegic, was a rebellious artist in his late thirties.
- Grace was a brilliant woman in her late twenties who had suffered a stroke while in medical school. Her left arm was weak and she was gaining back some control of her left leg. She had many problems with her memory, both short- and long-term.
- Kenneth, a college student, became a paraplegic in a car accident.
- Molly, a senior citizen with serious health problems, couldn't walk far or exercise much.
- Amanda had to give up her career in modeling when she was brutally raped and beaten. The beating rendered her a semi-quadriplegic confined to a wheelchair.

- Willie, twelve, used a wheelchair although he could walk a little, and had speech problems which made him hard to understand. His disabilities stemmed from difficulties in his birth.
- Carmen, in her early thirties, was severely disabled and became wheelchair bound as a result of cerebral palsy.
- Lorraine, twenty, had advanced multiple sclerosis and had to use a wheelchair. She was to be our dropout, owing to the strenuousness of the program.

Bonnie Bergin, as dynamic and dedicated a woman as one would expect her to be given the realization of her idea worldwide, spoke to us after dinner and warned us that we were in for a difficult training. Then staff members talked, and—friendly as they were—they seemed bent that night on testing the thickness of our skins, perhaps to judge whether we had the stuff it was going to take, and perhaps, too, to give us a foretaste of the training experience. Their strategy at the banquet table was to ask each of us in turn to speak and give our reasons for wanting a CCI dog. After each of us spoke we had to submit to a "miniroast" by the instructors—good natured, humorous teasing about what we had revealed so far.

Little Jennifer, the seven-year-old, talked first. "I just want a friend, that's the main thing," she said. "Oh, and somebody to do what I say." Are you sure, the staff members asked her, it isn't your parents, not you, who want the dog? Aren't you afraid to share your parents' attention? And aren't you worried about all the work you'll have to do to feed the dog, keep it clean, and give it water and the proper attention?

"That's what I want—somebody to share with. He'll take care of me, I'll take care of him. My parents won't have to help me at all."

We got a strong taste of Jennifer's inner strength in the little speech. If the staff was trying to see whether this little girl had the passivity often characteristic of those who have been disabled from birth, they were barking up the wrong tree (pun intended!). Jennifer revealed that she had exactly what they were looking for in a trainee—the will and ability to exert the necessary control to guide a dog in its service.

"What about you, Scott?" one instructor asked our new deaf friend. "Why would a good-looking kid like you want to be saddled with a dog in college? Seems like you'd be too busy with the girls to take care of one."

Scott had some residual hearing,* so he could hear

*Residual hearing is that hearing experienced by those termed hard-of-hearing that enables them to benefit from hearing aids. In Scott's case, he doesn't understand people well enough to do without an interpreter, especially in groups or large gatherings. Despite public opinion, lipreading is not easy at all—you have to be gifted to lipread well and only a handful of people are born with this skill.

Many words look alike on the lips. In Henry Kisor's recent book *What's That Pig Outdoors?* the title itself suggests why lipreading is so difficult:

During the flu season, I sat one afternoon in the living room reading a book while suffering from a typhoon in the bowels. Suddenly and prodigiously I broke wind. My elder son, Colin, then five years old, dashed in wide-eyed from the kitchen and inquired, "What's that big loud noise?"

Mystified, I arose from the couch, peered out the window and said, "What pig outdoors?"

My son stared at me dumbfoundedly. What pig?

Go ahead, look in the mirror and watch your lips: to a lipreader "What's that big loud noise?" looks exactly like "What's that pig outdoors?"

What's That Pig Outdoors? New York: Hill and Wang, 1990, pp. xv-xvi.

and monitor his own speech and was therefore easy for hearing people to understand. He preferred to speak for himself but to listen to others through an interpreter. "Hey, a guy's gotta stay home sometime," Scott answered. "And with that busy social life, I'm going to need a sort of social secretary—somebody to alert me to knocks at the door and all those phone calls from beautiful women."

"You have a point," answered the instructor. "In fact, a dog might even help you meet other girls during slack times."

"Yes, I'm counting on that," Scott told him. "Didn't I put on my application that I wanted a dog who had a way with the ladies?"

"I don't remember that," said the instructor, "but Paul here must have covered that on his application. He covered about everything else, maybe twice."

Anne and I looked at each other and then studied the guy's face for hints to his attitude. Was he joking or really irritated at the care we had taken over our application? The fellow smiled back broadly at us. "Did I detect just a hint of perfectionism in your paperwork, Paul? Can we expect you to ask that your CCI dog sit down not just *close* to where you tell him to but *right* where you tell him to?"

I could see he was joking now. "You got me," I told him with my hands outspread like a robber being caught.

"Well, that's exactly what we're after too—when you say 'sit,' your dog will expect you to tell him where. You won't be disappointed. *All* our dogs are perfectionists about their work or they don't get this far."

Almost everyone took the joking easily, and the staff wrapped up the evening by listing the ground rules of the training. All traces of humor disappeared: we were all to be *on time*, with no excuses for tardiness; we were all to be attentive and cooperative, with no excuses or lapses in attention; and we were all to show up alone, not with the companions who had accompanied us to Santa Rosa. Since the agreement stipulated that each CCI dog could have only one master, we arranged that I would be the primary master, taking the training alone, and Anne would participate by observing only. In order to promote a strong and permanent bond between me and the dog, Anne would not be permitted to pet the dog for a month (no one else would be permitted to touch the dog for *three* months). And Jennifer had to prove herself with her dog on her own, without her mother's help.

For a long time after the evening was over, Anne and I sat up in our sleeping bags and discussed our impressions by the light of a flashlight set against the tent pole. Maybe this wasn't going to be the piece of cake we'd thought it would be. We decided we might have to forego a few wine tastings and picnics on the beach. We were ready for the intensive training to come, but sure glad for our snug little retreat in backyard Santa Rosa.

Next morning, the training began with a film on the wonders of CCI. A major point of the film and of the discussion that followed was that dogs were happier as working dogs than as pets, and that most domestic dogs lived terrible lives of boredom, suffering from their uselessness. This idea provoked a lively argument, with Molly protesting that No, dogs shouldn't be pushed around but should be allowed to be themselves just as people should. It became obvious right away that Molly's attitude might prevent her from exerting the necessary control over a service dog, and for the first time I began to see how our attitudes about dogs in general were as important to the work at hand as our behavior.

As the discussion proceeded, it became clear that some of us had misconceptions about dogs in general and particularly of the useful roles they could play.

Bonnie then gave the first of a series of lectures on dog psychology, concentrating on what dogs really think and how they view human beings, and I think it was a revelation to some in the group that there could even be such a thing as dog psychology. "To understand and work with your dogs effectively," she told us, "you're going to have to come to terms with the fact that the dogs *want* above all to do well, that it really matters to them, and that they look to you for guidance, for explicit, clear direction, on what it is they can do for you."

In the middle of Bonnie's speech, Scott came in—half an hour late—and Bonnie looked up sharply. If some of us still didn't believe that we could be thrown out of the program if we didn't respect the rules, we were about to be convinced. "If you don't think thirty minutes of this program is important, you don't value this training enough," said Bonnie.

Scott looked serious and tried to reassure all the instructors that that wasn't the case. Then he smiled and said, "Of course, if I had had a signal dog this never would have happened, because my CCI dog would never let me sleep though the alarm."

After a second everybody smiled and Scott slid into an empty chair.

Most of us were eager to meet our dogs and assumed from the lengthy application process that each of us had already been assigned one. But it wasn't going to be that simple. In fact, the CCI staff had matched *three* possible dogs to each of us on the basis of our applications. That afternoon we were instructed to sit quietly in the lecture room while the dogs—*all* the dogs—were let in and allowed to roam around freely. We were asked not to pet or touch any of the dogs, but just to sit still and observe while the dogs looked us over in turn.

We sat in our chairs while thirty-two dogs of assorted sizes and breeds—golden and Labrador retriever, German shepherd, smooth collie, Doberman pinscher, Welsh corgi, schipperke, Belgian sheepdog, and border collie—sniffed around us and checked us out in their own ways. Some of the human participants showed some fear or nervousness, especially of the bigger breeds, but most of us remained still and impassive, hiding any eagerness or curiosity we might have had regarding our prospective dogs. The canines, on the other hand, expressed their personalities freely, and it was fascinating to see the range of those personalities. There were shy ones, aggressive ones, curious ones, playful ones—all very attractive and appealing dogs, since any problematic dogs, such as hostile, apathetic, timid, or hyperactive ones, had been screened out during the two-year training period.

The dogs roamed around us, sniffing and exploring, for about half an hour, and by then the more nervous humans in our group had relaxed and everyone now felt perfectly comfortable with all the dogs in the room. I loved the idea that this unstructured and prolonged session of exposure alone desensitized the fearful of their anxieties. It was my experience that most people who feared dogs never stuck around one long enough to learn the pleasures of its company. Here at CCI, that practice was reversed.

Now that the dogs had looked us over, an instructor told us to hold a hand out and let the dogs smell and touch it. This, in dog etiquette, was an effective introductory greeting. Once the dogs had that sniff we could pet them, and after that the instructors matched us up

with the first of our three "possibles," the three dogs the
instructors had assigned to us as choices based on detailed evaluations of our written applications. The mate-
rial we had sent in included a personality inventory, a
list of our own preferences as to breed, and an explanation of our particular needs.

Even though the three possibles had been chosen for
each of us, we were not given this information at this
meeting. The point was to let the chemistry between all
the dogs and humans express itself naturally. In this
way, we could all grow accustomed to each other's
presence before concerning ourselves with individual
relationships.

The names of the dogs were themselves terrific.
Eventually, the instructors led one of the three possibles
to each human. Scott got Peanut, Denise got Stanford,
Kenneth got Chester, Molly got Jewel, Willie got Victor, Carmen got Devon, Jennifer got Almond, Amanda
got Candor, Grace got Eton, Jessie got Colby, Catherine
got Webster, Douglas got Lancaster.

We had originally requested a German shepherd, but
the staff at CCI had found it difficult to match one with
me. For one thing, I wasn't the authoritarian type, and
German shepherds, it seems, don't blend well with
easygoing people. My match, my first match it turned
out, was with a Welsh corgi named Mel. This was a dog
Anne and I just couldn't figure out. I just stared at him
and he sat flat on the floor panting hard and staring
back at me as if he found me distinctly peculiar. Anne,
Mel, and I tried hard to be polite to each other, but after
a few hours with each other we had had enough of his
extreme British courtesy and gave up.

Our next match, on the second day of this procedure,
was Peanut, a small black schipperke weighing less
than five pounds. I kept stepping on her, and every time

I did she would howl bloody murder and then begin to bark at me nonstop. Her size was terrible for me—I felt huge and clumsy around her and started worrying that she wouldn't survive my footsteps for more than a day or two. Peanut the tiny just wouldn't do.

I don't remember seeing Chelsea in the room until Patti, the instructor, led her up to me. She was a large, beautiful black dog, a soft-furred Belgian sheepdog, very low-key and quiet. Frankly, I had been looking with admiration at the more "macho" breeds—the German shepherds, Dobermans, and other large dogs, dogs on the order of Lox. Chelsea was more delicate than that, an all-black lady with a fineness to her features. I had an instant of disappointment, but then I realized I had somehow been expecting to replace Lox, perhaps even to meet Lox again, reincarnated in my CCI dog. But that magical, fantastical expectation was only going to impede me from getting to know the gentle, nonintrusive creature the instructor led up to me. Chelsea looked into my face eagerly and patiently, but not with the assertive, grab-hold eye contact I had loved about Lox. Still, one touch of her soft, long fur and I shook off my hesitation and decided to like her. The two mismatches behind me, I felt we could be on the right track now.

I looked at Patti and she fingerspelled the name "C-H-E-L-S-E-A." I spoke the name and asked Patti to repeat it over and over again. It was a difficult name for me to say, and I kept repeating it differently, experimenting with the pronunciation, until Chelsea gently stood up on her hind legs and placed her paws on my chest. "Oh, my goodness," exclaimed Anne. "Oh, it's our dog, it really is. She is so beautiful. Oh, I love her," and she began to cry.

Yes, I thought, with Chelsea's paws still up on my

chest, this seems to be our dog, all right. And she appears to feel it too.

The instructors and participants tested the chemistry of their matches over the next three days and some new matches were made. Kenneth, wheelchair-bound as a result of an accident, revealed himself to be reckless, moody, and explosive. It looked for a while as if no dog in the group was going to suit him until finally he was matched with Chester, Chelsea's littermate and a patient, gentle, eager-to-please dog whom he preferred because he wanted a "classy looking" dog. Even then, it was questionable whether the match was going to click. Remember that old Groucho Marx joke, "I wouldn't want to belong to any club that would accept me as a member"? For Kenneth, that attitude extended to dogs as well as humans. Any dog who was eager to serve him was suspect in Kenneth's eyes.

The match between Molly and Jewel, a large white poodle, held up all right but it became clear to all of us as the training proceeded that Molly's attitude that Jewel was merely a pet would prevail over the idea that she was a service dog. Work and not play is the key to a successful relationship in the program, and Molly simply couldn't accept Jewel as a working partner. Jewel, on the other hand, quickly gained control of the situation—she responded to the instructor's commands with ease but simply ignored Molly's and sat sulking at the idea that Molly would have the nerve to tell her what to do. Whenever the instructor intervened, delivering a reinforcing bop to Jewel's chin, Molly would cry, "Oh, my poor Jewel!" This bop under the chin was the discipline method of choice at CCI, decided on because many of the physically disabled applicants were unable to lift, jerk, or pull—more standard training techniques—and because the dog's underjaw is rather tough. Molly was not making a good start, not good at all.

We began learning and giving commands from the beginning of training, and had to master ten or fifteen a day. Very soon we were divided into two groups, the hearing and the deaf, and we four deaf participants were to work with Patti Murphy, CCI's chief signal dog instructor. Our dogs had received the general CCI service training for the first eighteen months, and for the last six months had worked with Patti to become signal dogs. Patti had a cheerful, bubbly personality that all of us took to immediately, and behind her easygoing nature was an impressive expertise and a subtle understanding of dogs. She had grown up taking care of animals in her father's veterinary practice and was very involved in Sonoma County's search-and-rescue dog unit.

All CCI dogs learn eighty-six commands, and each participant needed to learn the same eighty-six as well as we knew our own names. But for the deaf group each command was accompanied by a hand signal the dogs had been trained to respond to. Some of these were identical to signs in American Sign Language, others were not. I was overwhelmed at the number of signs the dogs knew—Lox, after all, had responded to only twelve, and I considered him highly trained. We worked for six hours for the rest of this day, and twelve to fifteen hours for the next thirteen days, to master that vocabulary of commands. It wasn't easy, and all along I had the feeling that Chelsea was waiting patiently for me to catch up to her. She'd been in training for two years and knew these things backward and forward, but I must have seemed like a bumbling two-year-old to her as I struggled to remember the commands and to tell them apart.

Here's a list of the first set of commands we learned:

- The dog's name, in order to get his attention. The deaf had to snap their fingers. Those of us who could pronounce the dog's name correctly would snap and speak the name simultaneously. I practiced "Chelsea," checking and rechecking with Patti, until I was sure I had it.
- "Let's go." Means that the dog is to accompany you on a leisurely walk.
- "Go to bed." Used to send the dog to its own place.
- "Wait." Tells the dog to wait for you in an area or room.
- "No." Tells the dog, "Whatever you're doing, stop it!"
- "Come here." Calls the dog over to you.
- "Get dressed." Tells the dog to place its head through the collar or backpack.
- "Quiet." Tells the dog to stop barking.
- "Settle down." Tells the dog to quit playing around and be serious.
- "Go to your room." Tells the dog to go into its room or living quarters.
- "Release." Means, "Okay, do whatever you want; your work is finished."
- "Better go now." Means, "This is the time and place to urinate or defecate."
- "Go to the kennel." Tells the dog to go into its kennel—the special cargo box airlines require for transporting animals. This was a rarely used command but handy sometimes.

I soon discovered that learning the signals was only half of the problem; the other was getting the dog to respond. Denise, Scott, and I gave our dogs commands only to find ourselves ignored or stared at, seemingly uncomprehendingly, by serious, gentle eyes. But Patti would give those same commands and our dogs would respond instantly. "Heavens," I thought, when she gave one dog the sign to "do it now" and he dutifully performed his natural duty right there and then. "How will I *ever* be that in tune with Chelsea?"

The dogs' responsiveness to Patti seemed more miraculous to us the more we gave our signals on those first few days and met with blank stares.

"You see, it's bonding that's needed," Patti told us. "Don't get discouraged. It definitely takes time. The dogs are bonded to me, since I've been working them for six months, and they haven't yet formed bonds with you. Just keep at it, work with them constantly and directly, work with them as if you *expect* them to respond as they do to me, and you'll see, a bond will grow between you that will never be broken."

I remembered the bond I had with Lox, its special nature reinforced during that awful period of his illness. I looked at Chelsea and wondered how we would ever achieve such closeness without enduring a similar ordeal together. She seemed to be wondering the same thing as she patiently awaited my mastery of the signals that matched hers. But unbeknownst to us both, CCI had a means of fostering a bond that was nearly guaranteed to produce results. I called it the Great Seven-Day Leash-Up, and it would occupy the whole last week of training.

For the first seven days, though, we concentrated on the basics—the signals, with a little dose of dog husbandry thrown in (see schedule). We learned how to command the dogs to get up on a table to be groomed and to have their nails clipped. Anne and I were absolutely amazed to learn that the German shepherds in the group turned out to be the biggest babies of all. They cried and howled without stopping while their nails were being clipped. So much for preferring the macho types, I told myself as I stroked Chelsea affectionately. You never really know a guy until you get a glimpse of him at home.

A Typical Twelve-to-Fourteen-Hour Day at CCI Boot Camp

8–9 A.M. All the participants take a written quiz on the commands we have learned up to this time; then we learn new commands and how to use them.

9–10 A.M. We practice outside with the dogs to make sure we can get the dogs to respond to the new commands.

10–11 A.M. The groups split up. The hearing group goes to a public place, such as a store, restaurant, bank, or laundromat, to practice handling their dogs among the various physical obstacles they encounter.

The deaf group goes off to a special room full of various household devices (telephone, doorbell, alarm clock, mechanism to simulate a baby crying in a crib), with one person (behind the scenes) controlling the entire system.

Team by team, we review what we've learned and practice with our dogs. While one dog/human team is working, the rest discuss how to improve our relationships with our dogs—for example, by refining our body language in order neither to inhibit the dog from reacting nor encourage overreacting. The team in the practice room responds to the various devices as the controller activates them, and the instructor evaluates each performance—dog's and human's—

as well as the working relationship. Between devices, the participant rewards the dog with a bit of cheese and then plays a little ball to distract and relax the dog.

11 A.M.–12 P.M. The deaf group joins the hearing group at a shopping mall. We practice taking our dogs up an escalator and elevator, making sure the dog doesn't take up too much space on either side. The instructors watch us to make sure we uphold the professional etiquette geared to CCI's high standards.

12–1:30 P.M. We return to CCI for a lecture—for example, from Bonnie on assertiveness, or from the veterinarian on preventive medicine. We eat lunch while listening to the lecture.

1:30–3 P.M. The vet checks each dog thoroughly while the others practice under the strict eye of the instructors.

3–4:30 P.M. We have group discussions in which we review our concerns, questions, problems, and ideas, that have come up during the day.

4:30 P.M. We have a well-earned break.

6–7 P.M. With our dogs, we dine at a restaurant, either as a group or on our own, receiving valuable practice in working with our dogs in public places. Here, we practice enforcing a strict CCI rule: allow no petting of the working dog, since a person hovering over and petting a dog could inhibit the dog's vision and movement and, in the case of signal dogs, alter their responses to sounds.

7:30–10 P.M. With our dogs, we go to a movie theater, public performance, or other kind of social gathering to learn more about maneuvering in public and keeping dog lovers at bay.

During the session in which we learned about feeding our dogs, the staff brought out the animals' backpacks, specially designed in CCI's colors, bright blue and yellow. The backpack is the hallmark of the CCI working dog—the pockets in this specially designed belted pack are useful for toting, but more than that, the packs serve to alert the public that this is not a pet, but a professional working dog. A great transformation took place when the dogs were adorned with their packs. It showed they were highly trained individuals with a job to do, and all of us felt a new pride in our own dogs at the sight of them.

The arrival of the backpacks signaled the start of the Great Seven-Day Leash-Up. We had learned a lot of commands, a lot of particular rules and techniques, but had been practicing under the watchful eye of the instructors. Now for the first time we were to take our dogs home every night—a daunting idea in itself, but it was important that we fully assert ourselves as masters and forge the working relationship that would, we hoped, become permanent. An even more intimidating challenge, for some of us, was the physical one: once the leash was attached to the dog it was bound to the wrist of its human and was not to come off for any reason for *seven full days and nights.* If the dogs didn't know who their masters were before the Leash-Up, they certainly would by the end—guaranteed!

As I contemplated the task I felt particularly grateful for my own able body and found myself empathizing greatly with those bound to wheelchairs whose mobility and muscle strength were impaired. For me, I envisaged, it was going to be a matter of dancing around under and over the leash—experimenting and adjusting to make Chelsea and myself both comfortable until the next time we had to move, when the trial-and-error process would begin again. How much harder would it be for a quadriplegic, paralyzed from the neck down, or for someone with such muscle weakness that she was unable to pick up her keys without falling over if she dropped them on the ground?

Probably no other task so well demonstrates the CCI staff's respect for the self-reliance of the participants. I was becoming aware that in large part the training was designed to test just this quality—was the person able to *find a way* to solve any new problem that might arise involving the dog? Was the person able to not only live in incredibly intimate circumstances with the dog *full-time* but make use of the dog as an aid by devising and communicating solutions based on the learned commands?

Those eighty-six commands could be combined into an incredible number of problem-solving solutions—the dogs could be instructed to pick up keys, for instance, to take items off of supermarket shelves and hand clerks money for them, to push elevator buttons for owners who lacked the ability to raise their arms, to turn light switches off for owners who had forgotten to turn off the light before going through the elaborate going-to-bed process. In actuality, most CCI recipients made use of only about a quarter of their dogs' learned commands in the course of their daily lives. But even at that, for most of the motion-impaired recipients, the dogs made independent living not just easier but possible.

Still, to use the dogs both to improve their own lives and to afford the dogs a sense of usefulness, recipients had to live with the dogs intimately round the clock and build a relationship in which they were loving but directive. The Great Seven-Day Leash-Up was the first step.

CCI instructors and program directors knew that the training was tough and that this long last week would be particularly tough for the mobility-impaired and their dogs. For one thing, one must always guard against exhaustion and be keenly sensitive to the possible onset of illness in a working dog. For example, I remember the instructors taking Victor away to rest for a few hours when one applicant started growing impatient with the dog's imperfect execution of his commands. There is a powerful difference between firmness and unkindness, between the strict and the arbitrary. Here dog instructors were building dog and recipient to meet a hard challenge successfully. Never once were they unkind or arbitrary, because they define "success" in terms not merely of performance but of creative companionship where in meeting a challenge both dog and recipient feel pride.

The final week would fully test that idea. It was a little like throwing a nonswimmer into a lake, but the staff knew, too, that being oversolicitous to disabled people was not only insulting but, in this context, counterproductive. Throughout the first week of training, instructors had warned us constantly of the difficulties involved, particularly for those with muscle impairment. "You know as well as we do that when a person in a wheelchair enters a room, the people within see the chair first and the person second. *We* see the person first, and we're looking for your ability to live with and direct your dog, not ways to excuse you from learning how to do it. You'll find out soon enough that once you leave here with your dog, the first thing people see will be the *dog*. Then they'll see you directing the dog, and maybe third they'll notice the wheelchair."

All fourteen people in our group identified strongly with this notion and were determined to find a way to live for seven days with a dog strapped to their sides by a five-foot leash. The rewards were too great and too close to stop now, no matter how awkward, absurd, or downright impossible the task appeared to be.

Before we left, Patti gave special instructions to the deaf group. We were to keep our dogs from being exposed to any of the sounds they had been trained to respond to—telephone, doorbell, smoke alarm, baby's cries, and so on—since we had not yet learned to respond to the dogs' responses to them. Anne and I congratulated ourselves on our backyard-camping arrangement, which kept us separated from all such domestic sounds. That part of the assignment was going to be easy, but camping out with Chelsea, sweet and patient as she was, strapped to my wrist . . . well, we'd see.

In the middle of the first night leashed together in the tent, I awoke to the feel of Chelsea's cold nose on my face. It was clear she had to go outside, so I crawled out of my bag, unzipped the tent, and climbed out into the warm night air. The sky was filled with stars, layers upon layers of them, it seemed, but I was too tired to appreciate the sultry summer night. Fourteen hours of training had wiped me out, and I cursed myself for letting Chelsea drink so close to bedtime.

This cold-nosed wake-up call was repeated on the second and third nights as well, and I was starting to feel once more as if we were in the process of adopting a child rather than a dog. I dragged through the rigorous daily routines with that same crinkled-brow expression I had seen on the faces of my friends during the first few weeks after they brought home new babies. The white heat of late summer didn't help, and all day each day I longed to crawl back into my sleeping bag. But every time I daydreamed about the delicious end to the day, I was drawn up short by a tug to my wrist and Chelsea's gentle brown gaze.

I decided to give serious thought to rearranging Chelsea's eating schedule. I remembered housebreaking Lox, keeping him with me throughout the day and timing the passage of his meals through his body. I was even more intimately tied to Chelsea now, so why not take advantage of it? Scientifically, I recalculated when Chelsea should eat and drink, fed and watered her accordingly, and, voila! a full night's sleep! I felt renewed.

Showering, though, posed a different sort of problem. For that I went inside my niece's house, and I had to have Anne reach in and shampoo my hair as Chelsea stood quietly just outside the shower. It was really the most awkward problem I encountered and the one most suggestive of what those with mobility impairments must be going through. Most of these participants had been accompanied to the training by companions, so at night they did have some help in preparing meals, but getting into their pajamas or getting in and out of bathtubs leashed to their dogs must have felt like being chained to a great big patient redwood tree.

What bothered Scott, our deaf friend who had ended up with Peanut, the schipperke, was figuring out how to sleep with the dog. He just hated the idea of letting Peanut sleep on the bed with him, but as soon as he concluded that there was no way around it, Peanut hopped up onto the end of the bed, and that was the beginning of a till-death-do-us-part relationship. Tiny Peanut not only loved Scott but felt highly protective of him, and we laughed to see that little "David" proudly and courageously placing himself between Scott and any "Goliath" strangers or other dogs who might approach.

It was clear to everyone that Chelsea and I had not only fallen in love but were forging a lasting bond, and equally clear that the same was happening between Scott and Peanut. As the days went by, however, the instructors became concerned about what was going on between Denise and Stanford. We trainees didn't notice it, but the professionals saw an aloofness on the dog's part, a sort of indifference to his responsibilities, that signaled trouble between the two. What was going on?

A series of in-depth group discussions directed by Patti gradually revealed that while Scott and I had stuck absolutely to the rules of the Seven-Day Leash-Up, Denise had fudged considerably. The first problem, it turned out, was her modesty in the bathroom. Denise was willing to go along with the leash law within the realm of decency, but she drew the line at allowing Stanford to accompany her on her most private errands. She felt similarly though perhaps not as strongly about bedtime, and admitted that she had been removing the leash and putting Stanford in a separate room at night. Soon she was slipping the leash off during the day when it merely inconvenienced her—when she was signing, for example, and felt she needed both hands to enter fully into a conversation, or at home when she was cooking for her family—"Cooking's ridiculous!" she cried. "Nobody in their right mind would keep the leash on while cooking. For one thing, it could be downright dangerous!" Because Denise had a family to think of we were lulled for a moment into agreeing that it came first. Denise's husband helped with the kids, especially when she was at CCI, but as soon as she went home her domestic responsibilities started clamoring for her attention.

Patti, normally so cheerful and full of fun, became very solemn as she listened to Denise's explanations. Finally, after a portentous pause, she answered, "Look, Denise, right now if I were asked I would have to say that the training is a total loss for you and that you're just not committed to the idea of doing what it takes to bond with Stanford. The signal dog is not just a convenience, like an electric can opener or a food processor. He has been trained to serve you all the time to the best of his ability, and his well-being and good adjustment depend on your making proper use of him and relating to him with respect. His aloofness is a bad sign not only because it means you won't be able to depend on him, but because at this point he still isn't able to depend on you. Now, I don't want to flunk you, but it's my duty to warn you that you're well on your way to losing Stanford and being dropped from the program."

Denise was stunned. She never dreamed that the instructors would detect the subtleties of her relationship with Stanford or that her infractions could endanger her participation in the program, and she was mortified that she'd failed to understand the seriousness of the exercise. Bonding, and the loyalty that derives from it, is an essential ingredient in the dog/human team, and the Leash-Up, played strictly by the rules, was CCI's proven method of accelerating its formation. Close to tears, Denise put her signature to a written agreement stating that henceforth in the training she would adhere to *all* the rules.

On the day after the Leash-Up began, the deaf group began to spend a few hours with Patti in the "sounds area." This room was specially set up for the deaf and their dogs to practice in, and we had phone, doorbell, and knocking sessions so we could learn how to react to our dogs' responses to these sounds. I found this the most difficult part of the training, because we had to suppress all clues that would lead the dogs on the sounds we knew were being tested. That might sound easy, but I found it very hard to suppress all nonverbal cues—extraneous hand movements or inadvertent eye signals. Perhaps it's hard for all deaf people, who depend heavily on body language to get their messages across. This is true even when people are conversing in American Sign Language, which utilizes the face and whole body in its complex and subtle vocabulary. To some hearing people it may seem ironic, but in conversing with each other deaf people are often more successful and subtle communicators than are hearing, sound-dependent people, since they use the full range of communicative modes open to them—body language, facial expressions, and eye movement—besides pure verbal language.

At any rate, we practiced and practiced endlessly with the doorbell and telephone, forcing ourselves to ignore the dogs completely in order to encourage them to be more assertive in getting our attention and showing us the sources of the sounds. I suffered over this and longed to get past it. It made me nervous to think that the very support I was looking forward to in a signal dog was so difficult to learn to make use of.

A second problem in these exercises was to break the dogs' bonds to Patti, who had trained them so intensively over the past six months, and to convince them that *we* were the masters now. This wasn't easy, and every time a sound session began we realized with a sinking feeling that our dogs were showing *Patti*, not us, where the sounds were. Slowly, slowly, this changed, but not before I began to worry that it might not ever happen.

On Day Six of the two-week program we began to travel, the whole group leaving CCI on a bus (generously loaned by the Santa Rosa Transit Authority) and venturing out to one of the city's malls to practice real-life skills. Chelsea was wonderfully easy to handle and very enthusiastic about these trips; she especially loved going up and down on escalators. I started getting a feel for her personality—her particular pleasures, her sense of fun—as I hadn't as much within the confines of CCI and our backyard campsite. I also learned the virtues of having her be less obtrusive than, say, a German shepherd or other large, macho dog I had pictured for myself. On buses and in restaurants she tucked herself close in under the seat or table, fading into the shadows so quietly that most people didn't realize there was a dog present until we left. In this second week, my initial infatuation for Chelsea deepened with respect and appreciation as I watched her work for me and so obviously enjoy it.

As usual, the wheelchair people had their special challenges. They had to learn to use elevators and, where they had limited or no use of their arms, direct the dogs to push the buttons for them, to shop for them, taking things right off the shelves, to hand money over to salespeople, and so forth. These tasks took intense concentration, and Catherine, the ex-speech therapist with juvenile arthritis, got so caught up in the shopping process in an exclusive women's clothing store that she was horrified when she discovered that Webster, her dog, had pooped on the carpet.

Catherine, always shy anyway, was humiliated; the store owner was absolutely furious, and he rushed around the counter to bawl her out, making her feel even worse. Fortunately, the instructors were along to calm him down, but they couldn't help Catherine's embarrassment or her feeling that "I'm just not cut out for this." She kept repeating that phrase to the point where we were afraid she might want to drop out of the program. We all felt awful for her, and it didn't help to realize that it could have been any one of us.

As we discussed the experience, it became clear that Catherine had forgotten to use the "better go now" command regularly with Webster. Dutifully, Webster had held on as long as he could, but he just couldn't hold on any more in the store. "But there's just so much to remember!" cried Catherine, echoing all of our concerns. "Yes, that's true, and that's why we practice—and practice, and practice, and practice. And that's why we warn you to be prepared: all of you will have something terrible and embarrassing happen to you during your lifetime with your dogs. You'll be lucky if it's just one awful experience, and you'll be lucky if, as with Catherine, it happens to you here, where we can come to your aid. But remember. These dogs aren't machines. They're individuals with their own needs and their own wills. It's your job to see that their needs are met and their wills constantly turned to the tasks you set."

And so we learned the same two lessons again that we'd been learning since we arrived: respect the dogs as individuals and exert control as the boss. Both rules were designed to foster the well-being of the dog and working relationship.

Our trips into town, and especially Catherine's experience with Webster, highlighted an important aspect of owning a working dog, one that would become a major theme of our lives when we left CCI with our dogs. That theme was the public's reaction to the dogs, which wouldn't always be positive. A recipient of a CCI working dog had to be confident enough not only to direct the dog but also to inform and educate members of the public—sometimes against their will—about the rights of access for people with working dogs. Asserting one's legal right to be in a place when the owner disputes it isn't easy at the best of times. But for some people with disabilities, self-assertion is a profound problem in itself, so stating the facts and standing firm can be a major psychological challenge.

We were getting only the barest hint of the difficulties we might encounter with people who didn't care for dogs or who didn't want dogs on their premises. The reason we didn't learn this lesson fully during our training was that CCI is well known in the Santa Rosa area and the people of Santa Rosa recognize and welcome the trainees when they appear on a bus or in a shopping mall. We had the feeling that the whole population was behind us, and that Santa Rosa itself was a living laboratory for us to work in safely before we returned to our communities, where working dogs were relatively unknown and where we would be responsible for educating those with whom we came into contact.

One night all of us went to a double feature movie, and another night we all—thirteen, plus instructors and Anne, some in wheelchairs, with our thirteen dogs—went out to dinner. The waiters and waitresses knew who we were and made us feel right at home. Meanwhile, we began to learn the ins and outs of restauranting with a working dog: make sure the dog isn't out in the aisle where someone could trip over him; make sure the dog's not too far away to respond to your signals; make sure the dog doesn't take up room that should be occupied by feet; and make sure that no one pets the dog—this was and still is the hardest for me—so as not to distract it from its attentiveness on the job. I had to struggle to be consistently strict, and was ready to give in each time I saw someone say, "Oh, she's so beautiful! Oh, I *love* her!"

It took absolutely forever for us all to get settled and to make sure our dogs were well positioned—in this case, making room meant not just for feet but for the other twelve dogs as well. We were much too busy to notice the reactions of the other patrons, but they must have had quite a comical show.

By the time we finally got around to ordering and eating our dinner, we were all starving and somewhat exhausted, and after dinner the general feeling was that we'd accomplished a truly formidable task by making it back out onto the sidewalk. Nobody, not even those still not used to bedding down with their dogs, had trouble sleeping *that* night.

One other theme of our training involved discipline. The working dogs seemed to forget commands or signs sometimes, and the instructors explained that the dogs tried to test us occasionally by refusing to respond. We had to be firm without getting angry, never hitting the dogs but rather rapping them under the lower jaws, supposedly the toughest part of the dog's body. These reinforcing raps were to be accompanied with a smile, not a negative expression or tone. In this way, the reinforcement became positive. In fact, we were encouraged to express positive feelings to the dogs at all times and strongly warned against scapegoating the animals. "Ever hear of the 'kick-the-dog' syndrome?" asked our instructor. "The boss yells at the worker, the worker goes home and hits his wife, the wife slaps the kid, and the kid turns around and kicks the dog. It's a lot more prevalent than you might think—people dump their worst feelings on dogs all the time. Watch out for the temptation to do this yourself and if you feel it coming, nip it in the bud." CCI checks up on recipients and dogs periodically after they leave boot camp, and retains joint ownership for the life of the dogs unless the dogs are retired from service.* Where dogs are treated badly, they are reclaimed by CCI.

The kick-the-dog syndrome was one of a number of topics we discussed in the group therapy sessions that began in the second week of training. For some of the participants these sessions made up the roughest aspect of the training by far. Chelsea's breeder, Kaye Hall, who was allowed to observe the boot camp and who is a psychologist, talked with me about the purpose of having therapy sessions in the training. "I think Bonnie's theory in designing the group sessions," Kaye told me, "was to focus on the low self-esteem people with disabilities frequently have. Why would this be relevant? The natural instinct of a pack animal is to bond with the most dominant, confident member of the household, and Bonnie had to be sure that low self-esteem on the human's part wouldn't inhibit the person's ability to handle and care for the animal. The therapy sessions gave Bonnie a way to determine and help the recipient of a CCI dog to maintain and sustain the bonds they were forging with the dogs after they left boot camp."

This struck me as correct, although some of the participants may not have agreed, and some, I knew, felt that the group therapy sessions impinged on private issues that were none of CCI's business—for example,

---

*When dogs are no longer able to work, they are released from the "working dog" role. The master then gives the dog back to CCI and gets another dog or has the dog retired officially and keeps the dog as a pet. CCI doesn't encourage the idea of having two dogs, one retired and one working. It's too distracting for the working dog.

when one participant confronted another with something like, "What was it like to wake up and find yourself a paraplegic?" or "You've never told us what your husband thinks of your illness." Still, I found the sessions fascinating and revealing, though in some cases it took a long time to understand the significance of what we had heard.

Take Kenneth's story, for example. Bonnie, who led the sessions, seemed intent on eliciting Kenneth's deepest feelings about the accident that had left him a paraplegic, and the more she asked him about it, the more uncomfortable all of us became. Kenneth was a handsome young man in his prime who had been driving drunk when he smashed up his car. His friend in the car was killed, and Kenneth would always end his answers to Bonnie's questions with, "Why am I here? Why did I make it? It doesn't make sense. I was the one driving, I was the stupid one. Why am I still around?" The guilt and misery seemed right below the surface, blinding Kenneth to anything else, and I began to feel as if Kenneth wasn't ready to accept the responsibility for Chester. He was still too dismayed and guilt-ridden about having survived his accident, and that unresolved conflict seemed to make him unable to see past the boundaries of his own self.

My qualms about Kenneth's ability to assume responsibility for Chester were shared by other trainees and members of the staff. Although ultimately Kenneth did graduate from boot camp and took Chester home with him, these qualms were to be tragically borne out when Chester was later hit by a car and injured seriously. Kenneth had been too distracted by his unresolved inner conflict—which was much deeper than we realized at the time—to look after Chester properly, and this accident was the upshot. Chester was brought home to CCI and retired from the program. His pelvis had been fractured too severely to ever take the weight of a pack or a wheelchair again and he was left with seizures. The program and the instructors' constant evaluation were designed to prevent such eventualities, but mistakes were occasionally made.

Amanda, the model who had been brutalized, also came up for some very serious questioning in the group therapy sessions. In her case, it was not self-centeredness that was causing concern but a flip, angry attitude that had pervaded her reactions to the instructors in boot camp. Any time she had trouble with her dog, Candor, and the instructors directed her in how to handle the problem, Amanda hardened her face and became defiant—very often she resorted to the one finger symbol that *everyone*, not just signers, recognizes as the ultimate insult. If she was so set against the instructors and their obvious expertise in the treatment of the dogs, how was she going to act with Candor at home? Everybody was concerned.

At the therapy session focusing on her, she answered Bonnie's every question with an angry glare and very few words. But with every question, too, she drew closer to Candor and brought him in closer to herself—the bond between them and her reliance on him for moral support was clear to everyone in the room. At one point, after an hour or more of unsuccessful exchanges she suddenly drew Candor as close as possible with her arm and began to cry. "He left me, he left me," she sobbed—all of us deaf participants had to concentrate on the interpreter's signing to get this, since Amanda had buried her face in her hands.

Now, in small signs shielded by the body to indicate that Amanda was whispering, the story was revealed. "Things didn't end when I got out of the hospital. The thing was, when my fiancé saw what had happened to my face—" Amanda stopped to cry for a long time, and we all held our breath in suspense. As she cried, one hand gripped the fur on Candor's neck. When she began to speak again, Amanda was able to maintain a steady speaking voice—the interpreter straightened up and signed freely, without holding to the small range that confined the signs in whispering. "He just left. He couldn't handle it. Turns out it was the face he liked, not me at all. When he saw what he'd gotten himself into, and how much work I was going to be, and I didn't even have—you know, the face . . ."—once more the interpreter hunched over slightly and signed small—"he split."

Her shock, anger, and terrible hurt shot through us all, and we sat still as statues. Our dogs were motionless too, and the tension in the room was terrible.

But for Amanda, it seemed that a burden had been lifted from her. "So that's my sad tale," she said, wiping her eyes and then smiling.

"Now we can understand your attitude during the training a little better," Bonnie told her.

"What attitude?" Amanda asked, and we all looked at each other for a minute and then burst into laughter.

"You mean you don't know?"

"Know what?"

"I guess you could say you've been just the least little bit touchy during the training. We've all been scared to death of you, didn't you know that?" said Bonnie.

"You? Scared of me? You're not scared of anybody," said Amanda.

"Well, maybe. But we were starting to wonder if you were going to be taking that attitude with Candor once you got home, and we sure didn't want that to happen."

"You think I'd be mean to Candor?" Amanda asked

in alarm. Now both hands went to his neck. "I'd *never* be mean to Candor."

"Yes, but what if you didn't know you were being irritable, even angry? Like you didn't seem to know you've been flipping the bird to everybody who blinked sideways during camp?"

Amanda gave an abashed grin. "Come on, *everybody*?" she asked, looking at the floor.

Nobody wanted to answer, but fearless Bonnie said, "Yep"—fingerspelled by our interpreter to show us the slangy spelling.

"Sorry," whispered Amanda, stroking Candor down both his sides.

All of us breathed out in relief and smiled that it was okay.

Little Jennifer, at age seven, had some trouble following everything that happened in the sessions, but when it came to be her turn, she had no trouble at all answering Bonnie when she voiced her concern that Jennifer was too young to take care of her beautiful golden retriever, Almond. "Being a kid doesn't mean not being able to do anything. And being in a wheelchair doesn't mean not being able to do anything. I can take care of Almond. I want to," said Jennifer proudly. I was impressed with Jennifer's moxie in standing up to a roomful of doubtful adults. If she could do that, I thought to myself, she would certainly have no trouble taking responsibility for Almond.

Another participant whose ability to accept responsibility was questionable was Carmen, who had cerebral palsy. Her disability was so severe it was hard to know what she was thinking and what exactly she could do—in a way the effects of her disease actually obscured her personality, so it was very hard to know what kind of person she was. Carmen herself must have been aware of that, because she was very careful to take the time she needed to explain how she felt about her life and the role her dog would play in it. She was very difficult to understand, and the interpreter stumbled and mis-signed quite a bit. I could tell all the hearing participants were having trouble following as well. But Carmen refused to stop talking until she had had her say. The session was a long haul, very hard for everyone to follow, and I wondered how many people Carmen would run into in her life who would have the patience to stick with her through a complete conversation.

But behind the contorted mask that the palsy had created out of Carmen's face it was clear she had a very bright mind. Carmen made some extremely insightful remarks in describing her life and her particular needs, but it was her stubborn refusal to cut short her time in the session and the self-respect she showed saying everything she had to say that convinced us she would be a strong, directive partner in the dog/human team.

It took me a while to realize that the staff had left the three deaf participants for the end. It was their way of acknowledging an important distinction we three had been experiencing from the start: we, like all deaf people, saw ourselves as a breed apart, both from the disabled trainees and hearing world in general. Far from seeing ourselves as disabled or handicapped, we saw ourselves as representatives of a separate culture, the deaf world, a place so poorly understood by most hearing people that they barely even know it exists. Lou Ann Walker, in her eloquent book *A Loss for Words*, does a very succinct job of summing up this separate culture:

[Deafness] is a culture every bit as distinctive as any an anthropologist might study. First, there is the language [American Sign Language], completely separate from English, with its own syntax, structure, and rigid grammatical rules. Second, although deaf people comprise a minority group that reflects the larger society, they have devised their own codes of behavior. . . . The deaf world is a microcosm of hearing society. There are deaf social clubs, national magazines, local newspapers, fraternal organizations, insurance companies, athletic competitions, colleges, beauty pageants, theater groups, even deaf street gangs. The deaf world has its own heroes, and its own humor.

Many citizens in this "secret" world feel quite strongly that the only real difficulties caused by deafness relate to the existence of and necessity to communicate with hearing people (referred to by some deafies as "the others"). Were all deaf people on a planet together away from the hearing world, we would very happily go about our business, signing our language and using our ears solely to hold up our glasses! But because we must coexist with hearing people, who largely misunderstand us, feel sorry for us, and know nothing at all about our language or our world, it is our communication with *them*, not among ourselves, that is affected by our deafness. Thus, we live as members of any minority group within the mainstream culture— experiencing discrimination and frustration at the mainstream's lack of comprehension and affirmation of our life experience.

Denise, suburban housewife and mother of three, took the opportunity to put some of this into words when Bonnie called on her to show that Stanford would become part of the solution and not an addition to the burden of troubles. Denise was not at all comfortable with the English language but she was fluent in American Sign Language; she signed to the group through the interpreter.

"You're very quiet, you don't seem to want to participate in the group at all," Bonnie said to her. "Are your problems as a deaf person making you too withdrawn to take on one more responsibility?"

"Problems? Of course, I have problems. Who doesn't?" answered Denise. "But my problems don't come from being deaf, my problems are the problems of life—just like the ones everyone else faces. I'm not participating much because I'm eager to get back to my family and to put Stanford to work in dealing with phone calls, door knocks, crying babies, and so forth."

"But surely being deaf limits your ability to deal with the world. . . ."

"Show me *anybody* who doesn't have trouble dealing with the world. Life is difficult, and family life on not too much money is *very* difficult. It makes me frustrated to think that *you* think deafness makes me different somehow. Just like everybody else, I fight with my husband once in a while, I struggle with one kid in particular who is a real rebel, I worry about money—but I don't worry about deafness. And I have a very clear idea about how my dog will fit into my life. It's true that deafness creates a lot of inconvenience—but the dog is exactly what I need to solve those problems. Just let me get on with things—that's all I'm worried about. You think I'm not going to be able to take care of the dog or put him to work as he was trained to do? What am I if not a caretaker? What's my work if not getting things done in the house every day and helping everybody solve problems? Ever hear the term 'domestic engineer'? It's a very nice way of saying what a wife and mother does all day long, and it gives a little dignity to the job. I like it. If you think I can't handle one more way of solving problems in my household, you aren't seeing the kind of strengths I have."

Scott and I were way ahead of the interpreter in understanding Denise's little speech, and we couldn't help applauding while the interpreter was still speaking the last of the message.

As for Scott and me, we just didn't want to speak about ourselves to the group. By chance, I had found the lost wallet of one of the instructors, and I teased him by saying I'd give it back in exchange for having my group therapy session waived. No such luck—I had to have my time under the gun.

I spoke and signed to the group, and the interpreter repeated my words, since many hearing people have difficulty understanding my speech. I skipped over the question of deafness, feeling that Denise had clarified that issue very well, and went on to say that if there was anything that bothered me about myself it was my great ambition to work myself up in the university system and the dangers of missing out on other parts of life— the play, the fun. Also, I was struggling hard to show certain skeptics that I meant to make some large-scale contributions as a professor of Education of the Deaf. These were the things that I thought about and that I talked about with Anne and my friends, but Bonnie seemed to want to concentrate on deafness as the thing that set me apart. "Maybe you see deafness as setting me apart," I said, "but I don't—not at all. I see deafness as an inconvenience, as Denise said, and I see Chelsea as the perfect solution to many of the irritating details that interrupt the smoothness of my communication with people in the hearing world. As for taking care of Chelsea, I'm a dog owner from way back. I trained my last dog as a *sort* of signal dog, though now I can see what an amateur I was. But I have no problem with the idea of taking care of Chelsea and seeing that she does the work she was trained for. Doing the work you're trained for is what my life's all about—and believe me, as a long-time student and a teacher of teachers, I'm not one to waste good training or to ignore its importance!"

The group seemed to be satisfied with that and turned its attention to Scott. Scott spoke to the group directly, without the interpreter. He told of a highly supportive family and an enjoyable college career, and I could see the group lose interest as he droned on and on. The one interesting aspect of Scott's turn was Peanut's reaction: she seemed bewildered and alarmed that all eyes had turned to Scott. Her response was to get protective and to begin barking at everyone in the room, and as Scott droned on he simply took Peanut up on his lap and soothed her, petting her and reassuring her as he spoke. It was a fine demonstration of giving the dog exactly the affectionate reassurance and boundary-setting she needed, and I think Bonnie adjourned the meeting early with the confidence that she didn't have to worry about Scott.

That night we went to a live theater—an event marked by another round of protective barking by Peanut when the actors came down from the stage and into the audience as part of the performance. Later that night Anne and I discussed the group therapy session in our tent by the light of the flashlight. "It was really satisfying," I told Anne, "to have the chance to say straight out that we deafies didn't consider ourselves handicapped people, that our real problems with deafness only came about when we had to communicate with people in the hearing world. I could see the others in the group were sort of amazed, like they were learning something radical that they'd never thought of before. I had dreaded the idea of doing the group therapy, but it turned out to be a great opportunity to say something that hardly ever gets said."

Anne knew exactly what I meant. As a hospital nurse she ran into all kinds of people who misunderstood her hearing impairment, often mistaking it for a speaking or even thinking impairment. There wasn't much time to explain the basics about communication between members of the two worlds, so she often had to let the misunderstandings go and just concentrate on nursing.

"What I really love getting the chance to explain," I told her, "is the stuff about American Sign Language.* So few hearing people realize what a full, rich language it is, and if they *do* think it's a real language they just think it's English translated into sign."

"Things are changing, though," Anne reminded me. "Deaf people are writing books and linguists are showing an interest in ASL. And I think deaf theater groups are doing a lot to show how complex ASL is. Things

---

*American Sign Language is a highly evolved language, distinct from English, that has developed over the generations within the deaf community. ASL is as different from English and other languages as English is different from French. There is a way to translate every word, phrase, and expression into ASL, just as English can be translated into other languages. And, again as with other languages, sometimes there is no perfectly equivalent ASL sign for an English word or expression. Conversely, there are many words, phrases, and expressions in ASL that are difficult to translate into English.

I think ASL paints things much more accurately than English or other verbal languages in which words are restricted to two dimensions, whereas ASL is three-dimensional and not so dependent on imagination. The best book on ASL is Oliver Sacks's *Seeing Voices: A Journey into the World of the Deaf* (Berkeley: University of California Press, 1989).

are changing ... I hope. Look, Paul, I'm too tired to talk right now."

"Okay," I said, and flipped off the light. I needed my sleep as well. Tomorrow was the session's last day, and it was going to be an exciting one. I turned on my side and felt the tug of the leash on Chelsea, who was lying by my side. This wonderful dog, our new beautiful friend, was part of the shift toward understanding. And judging from my experience with Lox, Chelsea would go a long way, I knew, toward making the gap between my personal deaf world and the hearing world outside narrower and easier to bridge. I patted Chelsea and felt her sigh and then I fell asleep.

CHAPTER 3

Graduation

IT was all over but the shouting—well, almost. Training as such was finished, and it had been about as packed a two weeks as I ever want to experience again. But we still had our testing ahead of us, and even though I was a seasoned student I must admit I was a bit nervous about the exams. We were to be tested on everything we'd learned, from dog grooming through veterinary care and the commands.

Throughout the written exams Chelsea sat patiently at my feet, and I kept looking at her, hoping I could do as well as she had in her own training. Would the novice of the team come through to match the expert? We would see. At least Chelsea didn't seem worried.

After two pencil-and-paper exams, we each gave a practical demonstration of our control of our dogs and use of the commands. We performed in front of judges, just as entrants do in a dog show, and I discovered to my pleasure that Chelsea was in her element here. She seemed to realize that the blood of nationally recognized obedience and show dogs ran in her veins and she conducted herself with confidence and dignity. I found myself thinking, "Phew! She's leading me through this like a champ!" It wasn't the last time I'd feel grateful to Chelsea for her grace under pressure. There was something about this dog that made me feel I was working with a real professional.

The last exam was the real killer. We'd all heard about this part of the program but hadn't had a chance to think about it much. Now that it was upon us, many of us realized that we'd become quite accustomed to the group environment. Over the past two weeks, we'd trained together, gone to restaurants together, explored shopping malls together, gone to the movies and theater together . . . and now we were suddenly faced with what was called the Solo Experience. For the first time, we would leave the CCI ground with our dogs *on our own*, take the bus into town, and follow a list—quite a long list, I discovered—of detailed instructions before returning home.

When the time came to take off, Chelsea was looking more than ready in her yellow and blue backpack, which indicated that she was a licensed, professionally trained working dog. I was armed with a card stating that she was accredited by the state and permitted access to all public accommodations and conveyances as well as restaurants and stores. The final step was to pick up our instructions. I breathed in sharply at the length of the list. There were *lots* of tasks to do before we could return to CCI.

The bus part went all right for us, but it still demanded so much concentration that I forgot about my feeling of "being out there without a net." We'd practiced on buses brought out specially by the Santa Rosa Transit Authority and knew what to look out for in the narrow confines of a crowded bus. There was figuring out who was to enter first, dog or human, then paying and finding a seat that allowed enough floor space for the dog. Chelsea, of course, was used to these routines and always settled into spaces under my feet with

unflappable calmness. Still, I worried about her comfort
and whether she would be in someone's way. And I especially worried when I was on board with another CCI
team.

I once learned from a fireman that the thing many
firefighters dread when roaring off to a fire is meeting
another fire truck going in the opposite direction, since
one's own siren blocks out the sound of any others (it's
not hard to see why the story impressed me so; it's the
same kind of problem deaf people face a hundred times
a day). On buses, I worried similarly about meeting another working dog. Leash entanglement might sound
like a minor problem, but in the confined space of a box
full of people rocking down a street at thirty miles an
hour, dogs and people stand the chance of becoming
very jammed up indeed. Now, how do you watch for
your stop when you're stuck in a cat's cradle made up
of two leashes, four legs, and eight paws?

My first task was to ride to a shopping mall and purchase several items at a health food store. The instructions specified that Chelsea was to pick up the purchase
at the cashier's counter. Well, okay. If that's what they
want, I thought to myself. They must want to be sure I
an familiar with the full range of Chelsea's skills, even
those I won't necessarily rely on.

Next we had to go to an amusement arcade to play a
game of Pac-Man. I'd never played a video game in my
life, and somehow I felt both I *and* Chelsea were above
such foolishness. But I supposed that CCI had come up
with the tasks they thought would give us a chance to
try out our control and confidence in all sorts of situations, from everyday to the out-of-the-ordinary. At the
Pac-Man game, I saw that the point was to find a way
to concentrate on the game while still being able to perceive any signal the dog might make. Chelsea lay at my

feet while I humiliated myself with the lowest possible score.

Snack-time was next on the list. It sent me to a fast-food restaurant in the mall where I bought a hamburger and rested for half an hour with Chelsea at my feet. I saw Kenneth with his dog but held my peace. We'd been strongly warned not to interact or chat with anyone we knew.

The next step was to go to the credit office of a department store and ask for—and then *drop*—a charge card application. Well, okay, if you say so, I said to my list, and let the application flutter to the floor. Chelsea retrieved it, and then we went off to the elevator on our way to the toy department. In the elevator Chelsea maneuvered beautifully, positioning herself on my left side facing the door to take up the least amount of room.

In the toy department a woman came over to make a fuss about Chelsea, and that was hard for me, since I had to find a way to discourage her without being unfriendly or brusque. That's a continuing challenge for me to this day, but it's necessary to protect the dog from interference as it performs its work—and a significant part of its work, of course, is to remain continually alert to the environment as a whole. I finally said what I always say: "Since Chelsea's working now, please don't pet her."*

Lunch at a specified restaurant nearby was last on my list. It was a crazy choice, I thought, since the tables were minute—the coffeehouse variety with room on top

---

*Sometimes people look confused at that, so I ask them if they would pet a blind person's guide dog. (People tend to recognize guide dogs as working dogs more readily than they do signal dogs.) If I'm talking with a child, I ask, "Do you pet your teacher while she's teaching? We can't pet Chelsea now because she's working." They usually smile and say, "Oh yeah, right."

for about two cups of coffee. Again, Chelsea settled herself confidently under the table and I didn't really mind the feeling of her warming my feet.

I was eager to return to CCI to report a successful completion of my tests, but when I arrived I found a crowd of strangers milling around in the conference room.

As I talked with the others, I began to get the drift. Spies! CCI had put local volunteers on us as spies. At the meeting that convened almost as soon as I returned, one by one the spies got up to read their evaluations of their assigned work teams, and some of the participants were absolutely stunned at having been watched clandestinely. I scanned the group of strangers and immediately recognized my spy—the woman in the toy department who had come up and fussed over Chelsea. Hmm, clever, I thought. She had really tested me. But when she stood up to report, she made it clear with a beaming smile that we had passed our trial with flying colors. The only thing she was worried about, she said, was my Pac-Man score.

Some of the participants didn't get off so easy. Little Jennifer, it turned out, had cut a corner by asking a stranger to push an elevator button instead of directing Almond to do it. And Scott—hyper Scott, who rarely stood still and who talked a mile a minute—had raced through his tasks so quickly with Peanut that his spy had lost him at the mall. Both were sent off to do another solo adventure, and both came through okay.

One more event to go—graduation. I'd been through a number of graduations in my life, each one a celebration of the end of a truly monumental effort. There was my graduation from residential school, of course, which marked my jubilant permanent return to my family after ten years of boarding out, and that was a grand occa-

Back to school (for the deaf). Eight-year-old Paul must say good-bye to his Happy and fly off to St. Louis.

On California's Mendocino Coast, Lox stands tall with his beloved mistress, Anne.

Escapee Lox awaits Paul and Anne's return from work atop an old pesticide truck parked near their country home.

As Paul lectures to his students at California State University, Fresno, a casual observer might think Chelsea is asleep in the photo above. However, a closer look at the photo below reveals that her eyes and ears are in their ever-present state of alert.

E. ARIAS / J. MILLER

Chelsea provides "wake up" service.

"Hey, Paul, grab a towel! It's the doorbell!"

Dr. Bonita (Bonnie) M. Bergin, founder of CCI, with CCI's first service dog breeder, Jada (Abdul's mother).

E. ARIAS / J. MILLER

Canine Companions for Independence

Certificate of Graduation

for

Paul W. Ogden & "Chelsea"

Given this *24th* day of *August* 1985

Executive Director   *Board President*

Diploma awarded to Paul and Chelsea at CCI graduation when
together they passed the four rigorous examinations.

CCI STAFF

Bonnie giving a lecture to CCI boot camp applicants.

CCI STAFF

Bonnie and Kerry (with Abdul) working with CCI boot camp applicants.

CCI STAFF

Bonnie relaxes with her dog, Gravity, who wears the backpack for CCI's PR purposes.

E. ARIAS / J. MILLER

The top and only dog allowed in the restaurant, Chelsea accompanies Paul and Anne on their weekly date at Guido's Pasta Restaurant in Fresno.

E. ARIAS / J. MILLER

PERMIT NO. 02 8508 11
THIS SPECIALLY TRAINED CANINE COMPANION TEAM IS HEREBY ENTITLED TO ALL RIGHTS, PRIVILEGES AND ACCESS TO COMMON CARRIERS OR PUBLIC ACCOMMODATIONS AS PROVIDED BY LAW.

PAUL OGDEN
Participant Name

CHELSEA   X2A-179
Canine Name   Tattoo #

CCI Executive Director

7/91
EXPIRATION DATE (Void if expired or without authorized signatures.)

PERMIT NO. 02 8508 11
THIS SPECIALLY TRAINED CANINE COMPANION TEAM IS HEREBY ENTITLED TO ALL RIGHTS, PRIVILEGES AND ACCESS TO COMMON CARRIERS OR PUBLIC ACCOMMODATIONS AS PROVIDED BY LAW.

ANNE OGDEN
Participant Name

CHELSEA   X2A-179
Canine Name   Tattoo #

CCI Executive Director

7/91
EXPIRATION DATE (Void if expired or without authorized signatures.)

Paul and Anne's ID cards certify Chelsea's role as a signal dog.

W. MORA / A. TENSCHER

Lounge lizard Paul relaxes at his California poolside while Chelsea re- remains on the alert.

Chelsea's grandfather Jean-Jean with Chelsea's breeder, Kaye Hall. Jean-Jean's full name is Ch. Belle Noire Laxson du Jet, CDX, TT.

Chelsea's brother, Choucas (full name: Grand Fond Cyclone, T T), worked as a salaried ski patrol dog/avalanche rescue dog at Alpine Meadows, California. The ski patrolman is Bernard Coudurier.

Chelsea's father, Bounder, at a national championship dog show (full name: Ch. & OTCH Belle Noire Onward Bound, CDX, UD). Judge, Richard Renihan; handler, Teresa Nash; owners, Lance and Robin Willig.

Chelsea's mother, Tante, at a national championship dog show (full name: Ch. Grand Fond Amazone Noire, CDT). Judge, Lee Reasin; handler, Martha Fielder; owner, Kaye Hall.

Christl loves Gala.

Ogden family portrait.

sion. Then there was graduation from my local public high school, another important milestone, since mainstreaming for deaf students was unusual at the time, and maintaining good grades in an all-hearing school required some ingenuity. Next came college graduation from Antioch and graduation from master's and doctoral programs at the University of Illinois. Owing to the lag in language training deaf students often progressed more slowly than their hearing peers, and we also had to struggle against the sort of discrimination sustained by most minority groups. There were relatively few deaf college graduates in the country in the early 1970s and fewer holders of advanced degrees. The pride and sense of accomplishment I and other deaf graduates felt was immeasurable, particularly since all of us had often been told by hearing people with no faith in deaf people's potential that such lofty goals were beyond our reach. My family, who had never wavered in their confidence in me to achieve whatever goals I set for myself, had been unable to attend the ceremonies where I'd received my master's and doctoral degrees, and we'd all been disappointed by that, but this time everything worked out perfectly and a whole crew of Ogdens were planning to come to the ceremony at CCI. Though I tended to view the preparations with amusement—"Is the whole world going to the dogs?" I joked with Anne—I was awfully pleased at the idea that my family would witness that moment when Chelsea and I would be deemed a certified working team.

All thirteen participants had been excited for days, and at a certain point in the preparations we had taken a vote to name a valedictorian for our group, someone who would represent us in the ceremony and express our feelings about the training. The vote went to me, and I was very flattered, but with this honor from my peers came a stumbling block I was familiar with and had a great sensitivity about. The problem was finding an interpreter who would represent me accurately and fully and who could render my ideas completely to an audience.

On the surface, the matter of interpreter accuracy seems rather straightforward, and the training and certification program professional interpreters go through ensure that at least in theory interpreters translate everything *as signed* and everything *as spoken* with no changes, with no commentary, and with no deletions. Another stipulation reads that the information the interpreter transmits is to be absolutely confidential, never leaving the confines of the exchange itself. The code thus ensures that for the purposes of the work at hand the interpreter becomes more of a tool than a person, one that translates information into other forms but never affects the content of the transmission.

Sounds simple in theory, I know. In practice, however, it is *extremely* difficult to find an interpreter who is able to represent the deaf person's ideas in all their complexity. This takes not only intelligence and speed, but a subtle kind of understanding that grows out of nothing but familiarity with the deaf person's way of thinking. When my first book, *The Silent Garden*, was published and I was invited here and there to speak on it, I quickly found that using interpreters in a public context whom I didn't know quickly turned my carefully prepared presentations into disasters. The interpreter's calls for clarification and repeats continually threw off the rhythm of my talk, and in the question period I was often appalled to see how far afield the interpreter had been in following my ideas. A mess of backtracking and recapitulation would follow, and sadly I'd have to patch up things as best I could without being sure that my ideas and concepts and theories were really getting through. And never, I knew, did it occur to most hearing members of the audience that the fault might have been in the translation, and not in the content, preparations, or delivery. When and if deaf people do discover that their remarks have been mangled or changed in the process of interpretation, it's a terrible frustration to us that we rarely get the chance to explain and ultimately must accept the embarrassment, if not humiliation, resulting from inaccurate translation even where the original was completely satisfactory.

Let me hurry to say that I never blame the interpreter in such cases. The act of interpreting has built-in difficulties that are almost impossible to surmount. Very often I use women interpreters, which I consider an advantage since a person who sees me sign and hears a female voice is likely to remain aware that I am using an interpreter. When I use a male interpreter (though few men enter the field), the audience may eventually be lulled into forgetting that there is an interpreter and then be surprised by my "deaf speech" after the talk. However, the most important part of the collaboration is familiarity. If the person knows me well and we get along well, the chances are good that we will succeed as a team.

The idea of working with a stranger at CCI, however, especially in a situation where feeling was so high, and *especially* when my family was to be in the audience, made me quake in my boots. There were no highly trained interpreters in Santa Rosa with whom I was well enough acquainted to entrust my thoughts on CCI. So, although I expressed my delight to my fellow trainees for choosing me, I respectfully declined. Jessie, the wheelchair-bound special education teacher, was then voted valedictorian, and she graciously invited me to help her with the graduation address.

The ceremony was preceded by a dinner run by Beverly Coke, who had headed up a team of volunteers throughout the training. These terrific folks had set up lunches for us during our long working days—lunches we barely noticed (though we surely wolfed them down), since Bonnie would slip in lunch lectures, never wasting a precious minute when we could be learning about our dogs. Those lunches were a nightmare to me—try eating, watching a speaker, following an interpreter, studying a projected slide, and taking notes all at once, and you'll understand why I was completely unaware of lunch. Beverly and her volunteers were dedicated to the organization and not worried about personal recognition, but in retrospect their contribution was much appreciated.

Another volunteer group, one on whom CCI's continued success relied, were the puppy raisers, interested local citizens who took prospective CCI dogs into their homes for the duration of their puppyhood—for sixteen months—before the animals' actual training began. These folks just plain loved dogs, and they loved the idea of *working* dogs enough to tough out the hardest-going rough-and-tumble time in a dog owner's life and to teach the puppies obedience ... only to give up the dogs just when they were becoming reasonable.

When people volunteer to be puppy raisers, they are given puppies for between fourteen and eighteen months. Then if their puppies do not make CCI's particular standards, the puppy raisers have first option to actually keep the puppy. If the puppy raisers say no, then a home is found for the puppy. The waiting list for these "dropouts" is very long because they are well trained and have professional behavior. They are enormously popular. But as expected, all the puppy raisers choose to keep their well-behaved babies.

And why would a puppy become a dropout? There are many reasons. For example, it may simply not develop the bone and muscle necessary to tug on a wheelchair. Or it may not be assertive enough, or may have difficulties in overcoming a tendency to be distracted in a crowd of people.

Our dogs' puppy raisers joined us at the pregraduation dinner, and Anne and I had the great pleasure of meeting Chelsea's raisers, Pat Stewart and her teenage daughter Lisa, with whom Chelsea had lived for fifteen months. It was obvious that Chelsea recognized Pat and Lisa, but at the same time she showed that her bonding with me was complete, for her excitement and recognition were restrained and she remained at my side. Pat and Lisa, in turn, were absolutely thrilled that Chelsea had made it through the program—they hadn't been sure for a while that she'd shake off her rambunctious ways—yet had sad, sentimental feelings about seeing her new owner who would take her away. Through the CCI interpreter Anne and I were able to learn tidbits about Chelsea's furniture-chewing days— "Not our Chelsea! You're remembering the wrong dog!"—and we agreed to exchange addresses and keep in touch. I felt a lot like an adoptive parent meeting my baby's first parents, who were pleased to see their baby going to a good home but sad to let her go. In this case, however, there was one more set of parents to meet: Chelsea's breeder, Kaye Hall, who also appeared at graduation. All CCI dogs were lovingly passed from hand to hand with the confidence that they were headed into a life of satisfying service, but in Chelsea's case, at least, no one involved in her upbringing found it easy to let go.

Two hundred people showed up to see thirteen dogs

and humans graduate. I couldn't believe the turnout! So many people had poured love and interest into this program, and they were there to share in the joy of a job well done. When everyone was settled, I saw Charles Schulz, the creator of the *Peanuts* comic strip, and his wife, Jean, slip quietly into a back-row seat. I found out later that it was their first CCI graduation ceremony, and I felt very honored.

Since that time, the Schulzes have been important supporters of CCI. Jean serves on the National Board of Directors, and in 1987 she produced the award-winning documentary "What a Difference a Dog Makes!" which has aired on public television stations around the country and has been used extensively by CCI to raise awareness of the program and significant support for it. CCI has become an international organization with five training centers nationwide. If our dogs have a patron saint, it's got to be the familiar little white-faced squiggle called Snoopy.

Before the actual commencement occurred, the current puppy raisers paraded in the young dogs they had been caring for and handed them over to the CCI staff to officially begin their training. These canine beginners were decked out in their special blue and yellow capes—similar to Superman capes, actually—and, so adorned, appeared a proud group. Many of the puppy raisers visibly worked to suppress their emotion as they handed their charges over, and I began to realize that as many bonds would be formally severed tonight as would be formally sealed.

Now Jessie rolled up the ramp in her wheelchair to deliver the valedictory address. She and I had decided to focus on the packed schedule of the training session and to suggest that Bonnie and the instructors give themselves a bit of a break for fun every day. In that spirit, we had bought a bottle of bubbles for each member of the staff, and in presenting them Jessie pleaded, "We invite you to take five minutes every day to blow bubbles and chase after the most beautiful ones. Do yourselves a favor and simultaneously think of us. We'll miss you." Everyone seemed delighted with the idea, and Jessie and I exchanged a glance of satisfaction. Even this staff, who had been through the training cycle many times, showed a bit of emotion at our acknowledgment of their hard, hard work.

Commencement came next. The dogs were being held in the front rows of the audience, and one by one we were called up to receive them. I was called first, and I walked up proudly to receive Chelsea from Lisa, Pat Stewart's daughter. I could sense my family beaming at me from the audience, and felt my smile grow as wide as it could when I took the leash from Lisa. It wasn't *really* like getting married, I pointed out to Anne later, but it was *something* like it. The engagement was over and Chelsea and Anne and I were lifelong companions now. A family—and a working team.

Not all of the handings-over went quite as smoothly as ours, though. Many tears were shed, and when it came time for Candor's twelve-year-old puppy raiser to hand Candor over to Amanda, everyone held their breath as he struggled with it. It took a great many hugs and an awful lot of tears before he gave Amanda the leash, but at last he did it.

Peanut, of course, was going bananas. As well-wishers approached Scott to congratulate him, tiny, protective Peanut barked out her signals ("Someone's coming!" "Someone's calling you!") over and over again.

My family ran up and hugged us all. "I can't believe it," I told them. "Everyone here has such a strong feeling for what's going on. I think it means more to me that you're here than if you had been to see me receive my graduate degrees!" While we stood together Kaye Hall came up and introduced herself to my family as Chelsea's breeder. This was fabulous; I *loved* meeting Chelsea's "birth coach," who had donated Chelsea along with her two littermates, Chester and Crawford, when they were eight weeks old. Behind Kaye came an even greater surprise—the breeders of Chelsea's great-grandparents, who had flown in from Michigan just to attend the graduation. They and Kaye inducted Anne and me there and then into the "secret" society known as the Belgian sheepdog lovers of the world. These folks were so different from breeders I had seen with a single-objective "win at all costs" mentality. These Belgian breeders take a lot of pride in their dogs' intelligence, personality, and interaction with people. They brought a photo album filled with pictures of Chelsea's award-winning parents and grandparents, and a couple of T-shirts sporting a picture of Chelsea's famous great-grandfather Jet, a national champion show-dog and a frequent "actor" in stage plays. They ended the presentations with the gift of a subscription to the *National Belgian Sheepdog Newsletter* and the assurance that Chelsea was indeed a blue blood—a noble representative of a noble line of the breed.

In all the hubbub, Charles and Jean Schulz sneaked out unnoticed. I was disappointed that I didn't get a chance to meet them and to thank them for their support of CCI, but I guess they saw themselves as interested neighbors checking on a project they cared about a lot. They left us all to our celebration, and too quickly the evening merged into a flurry of good-byes. Tomorrow our class would be returning with their dogs to all the different parts of the country. Amanda was headed the farthest, to Ohio, and that seemed like bad luck for Candor's young puppy raiser. But wherever we were headed we were all beginning a new phase of life, turning our backs on our puppyhood and inexperienced selves alike to enter the outside world to try out our newly acquired skills. I hoped everybody felt as well-equipped as I did with Chelsea, the expert, by my side.

CHAPTER 4

Chelsea at Home

AS we drove home from CCI, musing about starting life with Chelsea in Fresno, I suddenly had a brainstorm.

I reached across Chelsea to tap Anne and get her attention. It was easy enough to converse in sign language while driving on the open highway. Signing in traffic was another matter—it usually couldn't be done.

"You know, I suddenly thought of a terrific job for Chelsea," I told her. "You know how hard it is for us to find each other at home? Chelsea could be our messenger—that would really speed things up."

I had always been amazed at how people learned to live with and work around the kinds of irritations, interruptions, and inefficiencies they couldn't do anything about. Boot camp had been a laboratory of such stumbling blocks and pitfalls, and the dogs had been trained to aid the participants over or out of the most obvious ones. But there is a whole category of aggravating details associated with deafness that no training program on earth could be expected to address—things that arise so often that if one notices them at all they are simply chalked up to the unavoidable annoyances of life.

I'm not sure I ever really thought about how hard it was for Anne and me to find each other in our big new house in the suburbs of Fresno. It was a four-bedroom house with lots of nooks and crannies, but we certainly didn't realize when we bought it that we would spend many exasperating minutes—sometimes heading into half hours—following a trail of visual clues to each other's whereabouts. These trails often petered out completely while dinner got cold on the table, a caller waited patiently on the phone, or a fresh idea dying to be shared grew dull and died on the vine. Hearing folks can find each other by shouting if they have to; deaf folks, as in all circumstances requiring the gathering of information, have to use their eyes.

So we began our first week with Chelsea with the intention of teaching her to be our go-between, and within a day or two it was working like a charm. "Go get Anne," I'd tell her in signs, one of which was a name sign for Anne, and off she would run to bring Anne back. We loved it, and soon refined the task so that Chelsea was carrying notes back and forth so the one summoned would not have to appear in person in order to get the message. Soon after that we refined the procedure again: the recipient would tear the note in half to indicate that it had been received. There had been too much scurrying around for pencils whenever Chelsea appeared bearing a message.

Now we had an efficient communication system that reached to the farthest corners of the house. Chelsea even functioned to give wake-up calls to one or the other of us when we overslept. "Get Anne," I'd tell Chelsea when Anne failed to show up for breakfast, and Chelsea would show extra enthusiasm for running to the bedroom and nuzzling Anne out from under the covers. I'd venture to say the Chelsea intercom was a good deal more effective, not to mention genteel, than shouting through walls and closed doors.

Chelsea settled into the house quite well after a sheepdog-type surveillance of the scene. She explored the house in ever-widening circles, always returning to Anne and me to see if we were okay, checking us as she would have checked sheep under her care. After acquainting herself with the floor plan of the house, she chose a spot to be hers: next to the fireplace, where our wood stove stands. It was the heart of the house for both of us, and now Chelsea added to the warmth.

There she listened eagerly with her ears upright and moving. She was attuned to all sounds, both inside and outside, and clearly made the effort to pinpoint their sources. Whenever Anne and I ventured outside, she was right there, obviously trying to anticipate our activities and second-guess our routine. The large lot with its tall trees was a source of infinite interest to her, but she remained alert to our whereabouts and ready to do us a service—for instance, by alerting us to the approach of another person or the appearance of a car. We were constantly delighted with Chelsea's eager responsiveness, especially as it was combined with her comfortable sense of at-homeness.

There were ways, though, in which her responsiveness was a little overwhelming, and we found that the fine-tuning of Chelsea's command system would have to include some deletions as well as additions. Both Anne and I are avid cooks, and we spend lots of time in the kitchen preparing elaborate meals. One of the first things Chelsea did when we arrived home that first day was to alert us to the whistling of the teakettle, which we had put on to boil as soon as we walked in the door. She also reacted instantly to the signal on the microwave oven, and her way of alerting us to sounds was quite energetic. If seconds ticked on and we failed to stop what we were doing instantaneously, she became quite insistent. We had a deaf friend who had trained his dog to alert him to the toast popping up in the toaster, but two cooks in the kitchen were enough for us. "This isn't going to work," we agreed. "We can't have a worried dog jumping around the kitchen while we're working. Too distracting."

I set about applying some of my training in psychology to extinguishing the commands priming Chelsea to respond to the kettle and the microwave. Every time one of the stimuli went off and she reacted, we would turn and pet her quietly, calming her, stroking her, and gently pressing her down to indicate that she should lie quietly. We wanted to convey the idea that it was all right to let the sound pass, to treat it as if it hadn't occurred. We tried to minimize our use of "no," and instead with as much gentleness as possible we stripped the sounds of their meaning for her. Happily, in a day or two she was completely ignoring the kettle's whistle or the microwave's buzz.

This didn't mean Chelsea found the kitchen out of bounds. On the first night there she made a significant contribution to the kitchen that we never even knew we needed. She started by nosing me in the middle of the night, pushing and pushing at me until I woke up and followed her, stumbling, down the hall. I supposed she wanted water and gave her some, but she ignored it and sat down in front of the sink looking at me, depressingly awake and alert. I wondered vaguely once more whether I had taken on a troublesome child who was going to improve my days immensely but destroy my delicious sleep. That wouldn't do, I told Chelsea, and I shuffled down the hall, climbed back into bed, and rolled over, ignoring the cold, insistent nose she thrust at me again.

So she went to Anne, and it was probably that night that she discovered that Anne was not only the pushover of the family but also the most intuitive one. The trip to the kitchen was repeated, but this time when Chelsea sat down in front of the sink, Anne opened the cabinet and discovered, to her distaste, a small mess of mouse droppings. We had no idea that a mouse had taken up residence there and might have remained oblivious to the little night visitor for a long time had Chelsea not been meticulous in her attention to detail. We soon relocated the mouse.

We settled into a very comfortable daily routine, much improved in its efficiency and general security by Chelsea's presence. Her main household duties involved alerting us to our doorbell chimes, a knock at the back door, the ringing of the telephone, the whining of the smoke alarm, the calling of our names by anyone, and any unusual sounds whatsoever.

Her favorite task turned out to be responding to the doorbell or a knock at the door. She loved to find out who was on the other side and rushed toward the door and then back to one of us with mounting excitement. Several times at the beginning she actually lost control and bounded into the arms of a startled visitor when the door was opened. Most of our friends and neighbors had long been aware of our inability to hear the doorbell and they all welcomed Chelsea's presence. It's frustrating for visitors to ring the bell and not be sure whether our lack of response means we really aren't home or we just haven't seen the doorlight flash. In just that way deafness can be understood not as a problem of thinking or understanding, as it has so often been misunderstood throughout history, but simply a glitch—or, rather, a series of glitches—in communication. These glitches inconvenience not just the deaf person but all those involved in communicating with him. But the signal dog is a living, breathing toolbox full of solutions.

We had a neighbor, though, who just couldn't accept that view of deafness or the simple solution Chelsea represented to the doorbell problem. Mr. Weiner, who lived next door, was continually befuddled by the communication problems that arose whenever we tried to pass the time of day. Periodically one of us would begin a friendly conversation, but we'd have trouble reading his lips because he was a mumbler. We'd ask him to speak a little more clearly, but at that he'd back off in a flurry of embarrassment. This was a pattern we were familiar with: people who are unused to thinking about themselves and how they communicate often seem to hate thinking about these things at all. Whenever we asked Mr. Weiner to speak a little more clearly or slowly, his self-consciousness seemed to make him aware for the first time ever that he actually had lips. He'd start feeling around his mouth, making it even more difficult for us to read his speech, and there our conversation would die.

But it wasn't only his speech that made conversation with him difficult. It was, in a way, a cultural clash in etiquette, for in addition to obscuring his lips Mr. Weiner could never quite bring himself to make eye contact with us. In the deaf world, breaking eye contact is the equivalent of walking away in the middle of a conversation—it's just plain rude. Most deaf people understand that the break doesn't mean the same to hearing people, but they still always feel a little surprised when the break occurs, and they look around for an explanation. Often it's the telephone—many hearing folks forget that a deaf person they are conversing with doesn't hear the phone when it rings—and they simply break off to answer it without an explanation.

But there are deeper explanations than forgetfulness for the breaking of eye contact. Some people just can't do it—they can't take the directness of the gaze. Every so often I have a student in one of my American Sign Language classes who is simply unable to participate because she is temperamentally unable to stay connected visually—scared to be looked at, scared to do the looking, or both. There's a feeling when that happens that what the person is sensing is an invasion of privacy, and when that is the case there's not much that can be done.

There's more to the etiquette of communicating with the deaf than indicating the reason for breaking eye contact. For example, there's the unspoken rule that one never stands with one's back to a window to sign (the glare interferes with clear vision). And there's the commonsense rule that says one must never eat or chew gum when someone is reading one's lips.

For Mr. Weiner, though, not only being watched but *participating* in being watched by trying to speak clearly sent his eyes darting and turned his mouth into concrete in the process of setting. Since we never managed to overcome these problems and have a successful conversation, he never seemed to understand that there were solutions. Therefore, he did everything to avoid confronting us while doing everything to remain a friendly, helpful neighbor. So instead of ringing the doorbell when he had a box of tomatoes or a plate of Mrs. Weiner's cookies to deliver, he sent his fourteen-year-old son Willie over the backyard fence.

This was mortifying. We'd be walking by the window and by chance see the ladder being maneuvered up next to the fence, and then, sure enough, there would come Willie clambering over one-handed, holding the cookies or something from the garden in his other hand. Worse than that would be the next step in Willie's procedure, which would be to go from window to window, peering in to determine whether we were in and where in the house we were. When he spotted us, he would jump up and down and wave, smiling and pointing to the gift. It was awful—exasperating and embarrassing both. We felt as embarrassed for Willie as we did for ourselves. The whole thing had to stop.

We finally caught Willie once before he got over the fence. "Come around, come around," we called and then we had a chance to demonstrate Chelsea's skill at alerting us to the doorbell. We accepted the strawberries gratefully and also learned from Willie that his dad had grown up just a farm away from a deaf couple who had no doorbell, no doorlight, no dog, and no way at all to sense a knocking at their door unless they happened to be close by and felt the vibrations. Mr. Weiner's father routinely climbed over *their* fence and spied through the windows until he had tracked them down and attracted their attention. Like father, like son, and like son again. Family traditions die hard!

Overall, life with Chelsea was shaping up beautifully, but here and there something happened to indicate that Chelsea wasn't at all a Goody Two-Shoes with an absolutely flawless character. We all have our imperfections, and from time to time a complete stick of butter would disappear from the table. "Hmmmmm—Chelsea?" and Chelsea would hang her head with guilt. Whereas Lox had been completely nonchalant about doing bad things, Chelsea was very bad at covering for herself.

Another habit that seemed far more serious to me was Chelsea's obvious desire to climb into bed and sleep with Anne and me. We had given her a blanket, which we folded carefully and laid on the floor next to the bed, but during the first few weeks after coming home from CCI, just as we would get settled in, Chelsea would start pacing and all but beg to be let up on the bed with us. "No," I would tell her, and she seemed to be crushed by this as by no other no's. She would lie back down on the floor and start fussing around with her blanket. It was a nuisance to feel her bumping against the bed and thumping around on the floor, but I figured she'd get used to the arrangement and settle down. She did stay on the floor but her discontent seemed to float up and hover around us. Once it became clear that the pacing and fussing were going to be a nightly ritual, we decided to write to Chelsea's puppy raiser, Pat Stewart, to ask about the origins of this behavior. This idea prompted us to gather as much of Chelsea's history as we could. Why not get the full story of our new housemate, from birth on up? We wrote to Pat and to Kaye Hall, Chelsea's breeder, as both had invited us to do at the CCI graduation. As it happened, Kaye responded first, sending this delightful and detailed account of Chelsea's mother, Tante, and her delivery of Chelsea's litter:

Tante's first litter: She showed the usual symptoms, especially digging a nest for herself under the deck of the hot tub. She didn't care for the whelping box we had chosen for her. One day her temperature dropped, and despite our efforts to be careful with her she escaped from the kitchen and wouldn't come when we called. Our four acres are fenced but we worried about her whelping somewhere outside. In looking for her, we found an area of fence she could have gotten through. We panicked and had the whole neighborhood searching the woods for her. Finally, I thought to use one of our other dogs, Pandore, to look, at first unsuccessfully outside our fence, where she picked up no scent. Then we turned Pandore loose inside our fence and told her to "find Tante."

She immediately led us to a ledge upon which we could see Tante, but we couldn't entice her down.

By then it was quite dark. We got out our sleeping bags and bedded down on the front deck below the ledge. At about 2 A.M. I heard Tante crashing down the hill toward—you guessed it—her "nest" under the hot-tub deck. We barely had time to force her inside to the unwelcome whelping box before the first puppy came. Then it took both of us to fight her to stay in the box, keep the puppy in the box, and give birth to the next two puppies.

Chelsea was third born. By the fourth puppy, Tante had resigned herself to the whelping box. She had eleven puppies in all. Eventually, we had her and the puppies settled and cleaned up. During the midst of this activity, I found a very large king snake in the room crawling in the direction of the whelping box. I am terrified of snakes but attempted to catch it and put it back outside. It scuttled into the heatilator lining of our living room fireplace. I called Animal Control for help, fearful that it might sneak back out and go for the puppies. They refused to help, so we attempted to block the exits of the living room with towels and wood. The snake must have found another way to get out of the fireplace, because we never saw it again.

Our troubles were not yet over. Tante was slow in making milk, and some of the pups (not Chelsea) were too weak to bottle feed. The vet gave me a tube-feeding lesson and we stayed very busy for a couple of days. Two of the puppies were getting colds and spent a couple of nights on Chuck's [Kaye's husband's] hairy chest. One died of pneumonia and the other recovered to become a vigorous champion.

Soon Tante was producing lots of milk. She took

her duties so seriously that we had to force her out of her box even to relieve herself. And she licked the puppies so much that some of their incisions for dew-claw removal [the dewclaw is like a fifth toe hanging off the side too far up the leg; it often gets hung up or ripped, therefore the dog is injured or infected] kept coming open.

When we had taken Tante in for her oxytocin shot [to end her uterine contractions], the vet had decided the pups were so big and lusty that he might as well remove their dewclaws then rather than waiting an-other day. I stayed to assist him. It was an eerie ex-perience because Fish and Game had brought in an eagle for him to inspect. The eagle was perched above the table we were using balefully watching the whole procedure. My nerves are rather taut normal-ly—it is incredible how much sound can emerge from such a little puppy when each dewclaw is removed. It was just too much when Pete [the vet] joked about what a great meal the eagle would consider a pup to be.

Chelsea, the third born, was the largest of the pup-pies at birth—6.02 ounces. Sizewise she quickly lost ground, and by six weeks was the smallest of the eleven—just under seven pounds. She was one of the first to open her eyes and bark at noise.

In puppy tests at five weeks conducted by a stran-ger in an unknown room, Chelsea already demon-strated an eagerness to explore and a readiness to come to a stranger. At seven weeks in a strange yard, she would also retrieve a newspaper wad partway back to the tester.

"Wow, this is just the greatest," I told Anne, when I read what Kaye had written. All adoptive parents must long for an account of their new addition, but few have the pleasure of reading one so detailed and full of special touches. The snake and the eagle lent a kind of mythic quality to Chelsea's birth story for me—and I loved hearing that her eagerness to work showed itself so early.

"This is fantastic. Get this," I told Anne, and I signed to her an excerpt from the letter on Belgian sheepdogs. "A Belgian catches on quickly to something new and begins to perceive repetition as punishment or displeasure unless a great deal of positive excitement and encouragement is conveyed by the trainer. Also, a demand will provoke rebellion whereas a more respectful firm command will obtain a willing response."

I loved reading this about the breed, since it confirmed something we sensed about Chelsea almost as soon as we brought her home. She simply hated prolonged instruction, and I even felt she took it as something of an insult if we kept at something too long. The extinction of the kettle command, for instance, was accomplished very quickly, and the creation of the "messenger service" in a matter of minutes. Chelsea was a quick study, and she expressed a kind of restlessness if we concentrated on training for too long. Wrote Kaye, "Repetitious training is more the type that a sporting dog thrives on. A hunter doesn't want a dog that will think on its own or that won't work for his buddies as well as himself. But a herding dog like a Belgian has to figure out how the sheep are responding, how to get them around and through obstacles, and so on. They respond beautifully to training, but the training has to take their intelligence into account." This explanation from an expert breeder of Belgians affirmed our intuitions about Chelsea's style of learning and reassured us in our approach to fine-tuning her skills.

In another few days Pat Stewart, the puppy raiser, sent us an equally detailed account of Chelsea's early days. She wrote much about what motivated her and her teenage daughter Lisa to become puppy raisers for CCI. She described herself as "outgoing with dogs and children, more reserved around adults, loyal and supportive." To my nonprofessional eye, this seemed a good thumbnail sketch of the perfect puppy raiser, and indeed Pat along with Lisa cared for many CCI dogs, quite a few simultaneously, before they entered training. The first Belgian sheepdog she raised was Breeze. "My heart broke when we had to turn in Breeze. I told them *I would take any Belgian, any time one became available, no matter what.*" When Chelsea came along, there was a full contingent of dogs in the household already: Friend, a collie; Teke, a little schipperke, "a tiny black high-energy dog," used by CCI as a breeder; and Sam, a Welsh corgi puppy being raised by Lisa. Here's what Pat told us about those early months of Chelsea's life, after Kaye had donated her to CCI to be trained as a working dog:

Chelsea was at first apprehensive. (Who wouldn't be, being brought into such a big dog family?) I remember her interactions as happy, loving, cooperative, not stubborn. She was soft in fur and soft in her reaction to criticism. *She loved to play. Sneaky* was an attribute that developed over the months we had her—it was her way of surviving as a pack animal.

Chelsea loved to sneak into the kitchen, put her paws on the counter, and grab whatever had been set out in preparation for dinner. At different times she grabbed (and sometimes consumed) four pork chops, a whole turkey, steaks, a twenty-pound bag of cat food. . . .

Chelsea didn't care if she was in or out—she loved to dig ... holes in the grass, holes in the rug, holes in the bedspread. One afternoon, she and Sam, the corgi, jumped on my custom-made bedspread, wrestled and played and *chewed* until it was destroyed. So much for matching curtains and bedspread!

Chelsea was the most destructive of the dogs we raised for CCI. She chewed a six-year-old, four-foot orange tree down to a stub. There was nothing I could do to stop her from chewing that tree. She destroyed a lawn chair by eating all the strapping off it. She destroyed a lot of our drip system by attacking it and chewing it when we watered. She ate an azalea and three camellia bushes and several rosebushes.

But she wasn't discriminating ... she wasn't just an outside destroyer. She dug a hole in our Danish wool rug and in Lisa's comforter. And when the comforter was gone, why, who would want the pillow shams, so she chewed *them* up.

She and Sam destroyed five stuffed animals found in Lisa's room by playing tug of war with them.

One afternoon Lisa and I left for *one hour.* ... In our house the living room was for business guests ... always clean, our best furniture there. Chelsea—was she mad at being left? Would she rather have come and thrown up in the car (she was often carsick)? Was she bored?—in that *one hour* she chewed the four white custom-made cushions on our chrome chairs and the arms and front cushions on our mint-condition Danish sofa.

In all the years of puppy raising before and after, *no dog* had ever destroyed indoor furniture. This was a Sunday. It took all my love and patience to keep her overnight. She went back to CCI for a week on Monday.

I am a single parent with extremely limited means. The furniture had been acquired when I was married to an IBM executive, and I knew it could never be replaced. Fortunately I found someone who could use the fabric from the arm covers to mend the holes in the couch. The chairs were lost. Perhaps it was prophetic. When CCI got their new training center and I had to sell my home because of financial reversals, I donated the sofa to them. It had belonged to the dogs from the day Chelsea chewed it up!

Sleeping arrangements. Do I have to admit this one in print? To get away from all the other dogs and rest she would get on our leather chair. No amount of punishment got rid of that habit.

I turned her in to CCI sometime in late 1984 after having her for fourteen months. I waited as long as possible on that fateful day. I had survived her habits and she was now such a great dog. I didn't have a whole lot more she could destroy, she was getting less and less carsick, and she was so joyful . . . it was like a little death turning her in. . . . I would miss stoking that soft coat, seeing those joy-filled eyes, having her walk so proudly beside me. I secretly wished she wouldn't obey them. I worried the training would break her spirit.

Of course, it didn't do that. But she was my baby . . . do we ever trust at first the spouse of our child? We assume *we* give the *best* love!

"Incredible!" I said to Anne. "It's like having a before and after picture—before and after CCI. She went into training a crazy, sneaky adolescent barely keeping herself under control, and she came out the ladylike professional we know. The only signs of the old days are the occasional snatch of a cube of butter and that restless pacing stuff she does at bedtime. Sounds like they never got her to sleep on the floor. Well, there's a mystery solved. Now we know that she's dreaming about the big old comfy leather chair. We'll have to do something to make her forget it or she'll keep on longing for it."

We gave Chelsea a special pillow of her own—covered with pictures of cats! She carries it all over the place—if we're camping out in front of the fireplace she brings it in there to sleep up near our faces.

Pat hinted at another problem that Chelsea hadn't quite outgrown when we brought her home: carsickness. CCI had warned us about her propensity to drool a lot and throw up during car rides, and it was true that this occasionally happened. We decided to consider *every* variable separately until we'd figured out some way of relieving her of this chronic problem. Anne's nursing skills and my academic, problem-solving ones gave us the patience to observe scrupulously and vary the conditions.

Sure enough, it started to occur to us that the sun shining into Chelsea's eyes was a contributing factor. We were careful to let her ride anywhere in the car where the sun didn't reach and disconcert her, since when it did shine in her eyes it appeared to upset her so much she didn't have the presence of mind to find a new place to sit. Often we brought her into the front with us, and we petted her lavishly, reassuring her all we could. Slowly but surely, that particular problem became a thing of the past.

While waiting to begin the boot camp training and before meeting Chelsea, Anne had expressed a strong desire to get a kitten and thought it would be nice to have a feline companion for our new dog. "Starting with a kitten, the new dog would get used to having a new friend along with us in the new home. Then the kitten would have the fun of growing up with a dog." This was Anne's reasoning. In truth, she really just wanted something soft, warm, and cuddly. Lox certainly had not been the type. A macho character, he didn't care for cuddling, hugging, or even much petting.

When we first brought Chelsea home, we would use the command "come to my lap," and Chelsea would put her paw and head on our laps. She loved doing it and we loved touching her soft fur—the warmth and receptivity of Chelsea. As the days went by, Chelsea would begin to respond by sitting beside Anne's chair and laying her head in Anne's lap. But that was only the beginning. Slowly, inch by inch, she would creep up onto Anne's lap. All of a sudden Anne, intent on her TV program, would find Chelsea completely sprawled across her lap. Thereafter, the command "come to my lap" changed its meaning completely for Chelsea. It meant curling up or even sitting on Anne's lap. With me she still just put her paw and her head on my lap. "Chelsea's both a dog and a cat," says Anne nowadays, "so we didn't have to have a kitten after all. In her former life she must have been a cat."

Well, if that's true, then she was a very large cat. But an affectionate one. Many mornings if I wake up early and crawl out of bed while Anne is still sleeping, Chelsea will come over to Anne's side and paw her, asking for permission to get into bed. All Anne has to say is "okay," either verbally or with a sign, and Chelsea will jump in and curl up against warm Anne. Then when it is time for Anne to get up, she says or signs "off." Chelsea slips gracefully down onto the rug and out to the kitchen to her breakfast bowl. As for me, I don't let her in the bed—unless it's freezing and Chelsea's cold nose pokes in my face and pleads so hard with me that

I can't resist. Three does become a crowd then. Maybe one day we'll have to buy a Chelsea-size bed.

Chelsea proved to be a finicky eater at first, and the explanation for that too proved to be buried in Pat's letter, but we had to work backward to it once the solution presented itself. She'd show interest in one brand of food or another, but once the novelty wore off she turned up her nose at the whole affair, and would then noticeably begin to lose weight. Needless to say, Anne and I became nearly obsessed with finding her a food she would eat, as we would have done with a child who refused to eat and looked more and more gaunt by the day. We tried everything, sometimes many brands lined up at once. It wasn't until we visited our friend Karen and Chelsea wolfed down not one or two but *four* servings of the food of Karen's schnauzer Dudley that we realized we'd found a key to Chelsea's tastes. It seems that since Chelsea was raised with very small dogs she preferred a small-dog kibble. I've often seen it written that a child is molded into the adult he will be by the time he's six. It seems that a puppy's first years are equally decisive.

As for Chelsea's drinking habits, this seems to be one area in which she used her training at CCI to meet her own personal needs. She began to pick up a water bowl gone dry and bring it to me for filling. When my brother Dunbar first saw her do this, he exclaimed, "Hey look! She actually communicates."

"Of course," I answered. "Communication is what this household's all about! She'd be out of place if she didn't find a way to get her point across."

We worked together on extending this behavior to her eating bowl, and now she carries it to the garage and sets it down gently next to the bags of food. When I fill it and carry it back into the kitchen, she eats delicately with grace and fine manners. Whenever we eat late or miss her feeding time, she carries her food bowl to me and lays it in my lap (Anne is more finicky about things picked up off the floor, and Chelsea sensed that early). Or she will carry the dish to us and drop and pick it up repeatedly until we respond to the vibrations of the dish clattering onto the floor.

What delights me most about these subtle signals is that they are so perfectly adapted to our lives, to our mode of living and our means of communication. There's a reciprocal feeling in our interactions that far exceeds the expectations we had when we first applied to CCI for a dog. Chelsea, Anne, and I interact as a unit, mutually meeting each other's needs and enjoying each other's company.

A measure of how well attuned we are on the emotional as well as practical level is Chelsea's obvious agitation whenever Anne and I have an argument. When that happens we raise our voices and sign wildly in anger, and Chelsea begins to pace back and forth between us as if to say, "Please! Please stop!" The first time we argued after bringing Chelsea home, she came up to us and showed the need to be let outside. We stopped everything, and I took her outside, but it turned out to be a false alarm. When we went back in the house and resumed arguing, Chelsea again signaled that she wanted to go outside. Finally I realized that she was trying, successfully, to interject herself between us and break up the argument. It was hard to ignore her, and her distress at our conflict only added fuel to the fire, but in the heat of the argument we tried to ignore her. Hours later, when we finally made up, relief showed in Chelsea's eyes and all through her body. She could settle down calmly again in her place by the fireplace, perhaps dreaming of ways we could all make each other happy, improving each other's lives so all would be calm.

In the outside world, especialy at night, Chelsea gave me a sense of security I had never admitted to myself that I wished for. When your eyes are the sole conduits of information about the environment, darkness reduces your certainty about what's going on. And yet I loved my country walks at night, and hadn't completely given them up since Lox died. But they held an element of uncertainty that Chelsea's presence canceled out. Her wonderfully attuned senses brought all necessary information to me as we strolled along under the starry sky—unsuspected traffic couldn't surprise me as we picked our way along a roadside; nor could a stranger suddenly appear out of nowhere. The sets of eyes and ears and that keen, keen nose solved the problem of reduced stimuli as nothing else could have done. But these additions wouldn't have made any difference had not the rapport between Chelsea and me been so finely tuned. Chelsea responded instantaneously to changes in the environment and I responded instantaneously to her.

Anne, Chelsea, and I loved to go on walks to new places, and when we went out to the beach or to meadows or woods, I was always fascinated to see Chelsea's sheepdog nature emerge into the open. Until she feels confident about her new surroundings, she will often begin to herd us along as a sheepdog herds sheep. This hearding instinct seems to be built right into the very bedrock of her personality, something that's hard to discourage. She begins by walking in ellipses around us, first going far ahead, then turning and cutting right behind us, then looping around ahead again to show the way. As she grows more familiar with the surroundings the loops grow bigger and she allows herself to sniff and explore on the outer edges of the arcs. But she's back very quickly to check on us and urge us along. Her protectiveness is so clearly expressed in this pattern that I can't help feeling grateful, but at first one part of the instinctual package wasn't so pleasant—when she was really ill at ease about the area she would nip at the backs of our calves or thighs to urge us along quickly. Sheep might put up with that, but Anne and I hated it and had to put a stop to it. Since we were dealing with instinct the behavior was stubborn and hard to extinguish, but we came up with, I think, a rather elegant solution. We simply gave Chelsea her own leash to carry. It keeps her mouth occupied and our legs nip-free.

Naturally, Anne and I were looking forward to our first camping trip with Chelsea as a celebration of the complete security we felt as a working team. We hadn't gone camping since that last disastrous attempt after Lox had died, and we missed it tremendously. Knowing Chelsea as we did now, we were sure she would become a seasoned camper in no time and would enjoy it as fully as we did. For our first trip we decided to take a short trip to a camping area on the Kings River. We set up the tent and went to bed, happy to be out of town.

At 4 A.M. Chelsea woke me up and it was obvious that she was absolutely terrified. My first thought was that there was a thunderstorm, and I peered out of the tent into the darkness. Nothing. I'd better have a look around, I decided. I called for Chelsea and she absolutely refused to move.

This was a new one—working dogs don't refuse to work. Their whole reason for living is tied up with their work. What was going on? I decided not to make an issue of it. First things first. I had to find out what it was that was scaring the wits out of Chelsea. Her refusal to accompany me meant that she was completely transformed with fear.

I stepped outside and shouted into the darkness. "Hey! Anybody there? Hey! Are you there???" Let me admit right out that this wasn't easy. My knees were knocking and I expected somebody or something to leap out of the darkness at any second. The last thing I hoped for was an answer—a physical answer—to my calls. When there was none I sighed with relief and gave up, even though Chelsea still stood shaking at the flap of the tent, barely daring to peer out at me as I risked, if not my life, then surely my dignity.

When I climbed back into my sleeping bag Chelsea crawled up as close to me as she could, and I decided that she was just not used to the experience of sleeping outdoors. She stayed pushed up against me, but I could feel she wasn't relaxed. Every two or three minutes she lifted her head, went tense, and perked up her ears. I went out again, but all was calm, dark, and motionless. Finally I fell back to sleep and Chelsea did too, I suppose.

The next morning Anne and I tried to solve the mystery by introducing ourselves and striking up a conversation with the campers in the tent next to ours. When we told them about Chelsea's mysterious fright in the night, the man nodded sagely. "Oh, yes, indeed," he said. "Scared you, did it?" he asked Chelsea. He was a large, friendly man, but slow to come to the point. "Well, yes, I heard it myself. One of the world's most beautiful sounds and one of the world's eeriest sounds. If you'll excuse me."

He seemed suddenly embarrassed at mentioning "sounds" to a deaf person, but I was used to that, and we were dying of curiosity. "What sound?" I persisted.

Reassured that he wouldn't insult us by referring to

something outside our experience, he finally put us out of our misery. "Coyotes. A couple of 'em. They were howling out there at each other last night to beat the band."

"What time was that?" I asked him.

"Oh, 'bout four o'clock. Woke me up. I listened to 'em for maybe half an hour. Long, eerie, crying sounds meant to travel over long distances. Some people think they sound like dogs singing, some like dogs crying, some nothing like dogs at all. Sure can scare you, I suppose, if you don't know what they are."

And especially if your job is to alert your companions to the sounds of the environment. And especially if your instinct tells you that not only informing but *protecting* is part of your job. And *especially* if you're a dog and the sound you hear sounds a little like a dog and then not quite like a dog. . . . No wonder Chelsea was terrified. She must have thought she'd been transplanted to another world.

"Funny part was, then I heard you. Heard you shouting your head off out there at the coyotes. I stuck my head out and yelled as loud as *I* could, saying, 'Repeat what you said. I didn't understand.' But you just kept on shouting at those coyotes. I found it pretty strange, I can tell you."

It struck me as funny—so funny I began to laugh. It would have been hard to explain to our new acquaintances just exactly what was so comical, but they seemed to enjoy the idea of such commotion suddenly erupting in the peaceful wee hours in the wilderness.

The excitement in the night amused me, but what really had me laughing was the idea that we had felt so completely secure, so completely protected, and so linked up with the world outside—even more completely than any hearing person might have felt. But no one, I realized as I laughed, is immune to the world's mysteries and dangers, imagined or real—not even Chelsea. And nothing, not even Chelsea, could bring back life "the way it used to be with Lox." We were going to have to have patience while Chelsea learned the hidden pleasure of camping, just as she had waited patiently for us to learn our eighty-six commands. She slowly did learn, though, just as we had. Chelsea wasn't macho like Lox; she was more ladylike and cautious. But Anne always slept like a baby on our camping trips, with Chelsea and her radar ears nearby.

CHAPTER 5

Dog about Town

LIFE with Chelsea encompassed town as well as country, and our excursions into the city were often a source of excitement for her. But early on, if we encountered an emergency vehicle with its siren on, Chelsea's extreme responsiveness left Anne and me practically nervous wrecks, for Chelsea reacted as if the world was suddenly coming to an end. Like most deaf people, Anne and I are extremely vigilant drivers, always alert to flashing red lights both ahead of us and approaching from behind. But whenever Chelsea would react to a siren by pushing, pushing, pushing at our elbows with her nose, we'd suddenly be responding to the siren *and* having to reassure Chelsea, who would get increasingly nervous as the siren grew louder. As we struggled to calm her while trying to pull over to the side of the road, it always seemed as if we were just an inch away from a traffic accident, and when the siren had passed I found myself having to sit still for several minutes just to cool down. This was no good—here was a behavior that had to be extinguished, and we worked on it persistently until Chelsea began to meet any siren with a blessed lack of concern.

The Fresno Fashion Fair Mall was heaven for Chelsea, with all its associations to our old CCI stomping grounds. The bright lights and brisk comings and goings—all these clearly excited Chelsea, but they were nothing compared to the escalators. She loved those escalators, and rode them with a wagging tail and obvious enjoyment of the attention she aroused. Children especially loved to see her all decked out to go shopping in her working dog backpack—one of the professors at school called her "the walking briefcase"—and more than once we sensed a commotion only to discover upon looking around that we were the center of attention.

At first, though, we weren't so sure that our shopping excursions in Fresno were going to measure up to those in Santa Rosa, where almost everybody was used to seeing working dogs in places of business. As the CCI dog instructors had emphasized, one of our important responsibilities was to educate the public to the legal access rights of working dogs in public places. "Not everybody is a dog lover," said Bonnie. "Some people just hate dogs or are deathly afraid of them. Some people consider dogs dirty and take offense at their presence around new merchandise or food. You're going to have to be a diplomat and an educator rolled into one, because you'll need to assert your rights and prove them—with your ID card, if necessary, but with the kind of friendly, nonthreatening style that will make people *want* to welcome you." Santa Rosa, we knew, was full of people who knew all about working dogs' rights of access, but how would Fresno feel about admitting a dog to its stores and restaurants?

As it happened, we met no resistance whatsoever at the mall. The first time we went we met a security guard named Bill. He stopped us and we explained the concept of working dogs and showed him our ID card. He apparently alerted the entire security staff about us, and they must have told the merchants. We never had anything but a friendly reception anywhere in the mall. The same was generally true almost everywhere in the city. An exception, though, was my first visit to a particular grocery store in town.

Chelsea and I stepped inside F & G Grocery, and I was prepared to show my card and explain working dogs should anybody stop me. What I hadn't counted on, though, was a language problem. All the personnel at F & G were Vietnamese, and none of them seemed to speak English, or at least not well enough to understand me. Deafness and hard-to-understand speech are big enough stumbling blocks to deaf/hearing communication. Throw up another obstacle, such as a language barrier, and things can get ridiculous.

The clerk who stopped me, undoubtedly experienced in such communications snaggles with her customers due to her inability to speak English, resorted to the most efficient solution. She pointed at Chelsea and then pointed to the door; then, with a scowl on her face, she did it again. She didn't even have to try to speak her message. It was coming in visually, loud and clear. "No dogs are allowed."

I smiled, handed her the ID card and said, "It is lawful." She shrugged, then pointed us out the door again. *I* pointed to the card and then scribbled a note: "It is lawful." She shrugged, then pointed us out the door . . . again.

I looked up, hoping to find someone who spoke English who would step forward and help. Eyes were looking at me from all around the store. Nobody was smiling. Even the children were staring at me solemnly, wondering what was going to happen. Suddenly I wanted to give up and run out, but I realized that up to now I had had it easy. Everybody had loved and welcomed Chelsea in my neighborhood, at the university, and about town because they had the information they needed. Here was a perfect example of an effort stalled by blocked information. This was what my work as teacher of teachers of the deaf was all about. In my books, lectures, and classes, my constant theme was that deafness was not a handicap but a serious inconvenience that could be overcome by finding new ways to channel information. Was I going to fly from a simple little problem just because I'd come up against one brick wall in the form of a language barrier?

I vowed to smile through my extreme self-consciousness and point to the note I'd written again. "It's legal" was the information I needed to convey. I resolved to do a charade if I had to.

The clerk took my note and the ID card and went into the back room. Chelsea and I stood there waiting, and I noticed a happy grin on her face. She was loving the attention; I was hating it.

When the clerk returned she refused to look at me but pointed once again to Chelsea and then to the door. There was going to be no compromise.

Now I had to advance to the next level of meaning: consequences. "You are breaking the law," I said. "Do you want to go to jail?" I don't know if she understood my words but she surely understood I wasn't going to give up. She picked up my ID card and went into the back room once more. I stood there sweating, but smiled at the crowd. Nobody smiled back.

Finally, the clerk reemerged. She handed me the ID card and with a cock of her head indicated that Chelsea and I could enter the aisles. But as I thanked her she pointed to her eye and then at Chelsea—fiercely. "Keep an eye on that dog," she was saying, in no uncertain terms.

Well, good. I had triumphed. Everyone resumed their

shopping and I stood there trying to remember what on earth I'd come in for. My entire shopping list had flown right out of my mind. I just wandered down the aisles hoping something would jog my memory, but as I began my stroll I noticed a man keeping pace with me and eyeing me over the top of the aisle. This must have been the decision maker from the back room. He watched every move I made, never letting me out of his sight. Suddenly I felt that, right in my own home town, I was in a foreign land where I was completely mistrusted. What the people in the market expected or feared Chelsea might do I had no idea, but I decided not to upset them or myself any longer. I waved to the man across the top of the aisle—which put him further on his guard—grabbed something, anything, off the shelf, paid for it, and ran. I'd done what I'd set out to do, I'd won my victory; but I felt just terrible about the whole thing. The distrust I'd met with unsettled me, and I felt that in spite of my "victory" I had failed in conveying important information, both about deafness and working dogs.

A few days later, one of my star students came rushing up to me after class and began apologizing profusely for my treatment in the store. She worked there as a checkout clerk and had been off the day I went in, but immediately recognized me when her coworkers described the incident. And of course, she had recognized Chelsea, who often came to class with me and curled up quietly in the corner throughout the hour. She was mortified at how I had been treated and had explained to the workers at the store that I was her professor at the university and that my dog was a professionally trained and licensed working dog that had every right to be there. Everyone felt awful about it—embarrassed and ashamed. So the message finally worked its way through, with a little help from a translator. (Some time later, Chelsea and I met with the same dubious reception at the wedding of the same young lady. I could virtually *feel* the outrage behind the stares: who on earth was nervy enough to bring a dog to a wedding? But when the bride insisted on being photographed with Chelsea—not once, but in many different poses— Chelsea became a star and I a thoroughly welcome guest.)

The incident at the grocery store was the exception to the rule, however. Most business people in Fresno welcomed Chelsea and often tried to make friends with her. That was strictly against the rules—working dogs have a job to do, are not pets, and must not be distracted from their alertness to the surroundings. I tried very hard to enforce this, but it was always difficult for me to discourage friendly gestures to my dog. One enterprising counter worker at Burger King, however, managed to get around the rule. He was a very serious young man who seemed completely oblivious to Chelsea's presence. He handed me my order, and I didn't notice until I reached the table that there was another bag on my tray. The young man hadn't made any attempt to be friendly or even looked at us as we walked away, but the bag was clearly not a mistake. It contained a handful of Milk-Bone biscuits, with compliments from a friend.

People on the university campus loved the idea that Chelsea would let me know when somebody called my name and then lead me to the caller. Perhaps their being students and professors, committed to the quest for truth, made them eager to see this phenomenon for themselves. In the first months after acquiring Chelsea I couldn't walk across the campus without being stopped every few yards to respond to a call. I imagined that just before these friendly callers hollered my name they would nudge their companion in the ribs and say, "Watch this!" Then, "Paul!" they'd yell, and Chelsea would stop and lead me over.

Incredible! All of a sudden I was the most popular guy on campus. But when I'd stop to chat, I'd find the caller to be a complete stranger, somebody who'd heard of Chelsea and wanted to see her in action. This person would then commence to describe what he or she knew about Chelsea and the companion would listen open-mouthed while I stood and glanced at my watch. I was proud of Chelsea and glad to see she was making such a name for herself—I considered it good PR for working dogs to be seen and understood by as many people as possible. But the gist of these encounters was getting pretty repetitive, and my days were being frittered away by people I didn't even know stopping me.

Not only that, I was nervous about too *much* fame. Poor Lox had been the near-victim of a nutty student carrying a BB gun and stalking the dog who'd bitten him. Owing to Lox's fame and high visibility on campus, this furious student decided Lox had been his tormentor. The security police disarmed the man and cleared Lox's good name, but the incident made me nervous. I was all for Chelsea becoming well known, but I wanted to make sure she was treated respectfully, as the reliable, professional working dog she was—not as a curiosity.

"The people who call out to me just want to see Chelsea perform," I told Anne. "It's amazing how interesting they find her. But they seem oblivious to the fact that there's a busy man with classes to teach and meetings to attend on the other end of the leash. It's getting so I get stopped maybe five, six times between my office and the cafeteria. It's becoming a real problem, and I can hardly keep my impatience from showing."

It was a classic case of a very useful CCI command having unexpected consequences. We decided there was nothing for it but to retrain Chelsea to respond not to my name but to a secret password known only to Anne. People who really wanted to talk with me would find another way to get my attention, and hopefully the rest would stop treating Chelsea and me as a dog and pony show. ("I guess," I told Anne, "that makes me the pony!")

But eventually we became careless about our secret password and it leaked out. One day Chelsea stopped me in our trek across campus and turned to lead me to a caller. I of course expected to see Anne, but there was Carla, a graduate student friend with her own little signal dog, Questor. No harm done, I thought, as Carla and I chatted casually—but a group of new faculty members standing nearby picked up the password. From that day forward, my passage around and about once more became a matter of fits and starts. Exasperated, I changed the password, and Anne and I kept closer tabs on it this time.

I was always glad to see Carla and Questor. Carla was an attractive, easygoing young woman who had lost her hearing in her teens, and Questor—a little Welsh corgi, also from CCI—was a laid-back type as well. Where Chelsea was obviously alert and eager to work, her most characteristic pose being sitting to attention with her ears raised, Questor was a lot lower to the ground, both in body type and personality. Together Carla and Questor strolled across campus as if out for a constitutional. Occasionally we would bump into each other and swap dog stories. Some of the stories she had to tell were polar opposites of my experiences.

When I told Carla of my exasperating start-and-stop travels around school, she came back with a story from the other end of the spectrum. Far from having to contend with too much friendliness and acceptance, she was continually meeting with resistance. She just couldn't get the security guards at the mall—those same guards who had accepted Chelsea so easily—from stopping her and giving her a hard time about bringing Questor into the no-dog shopping area. Every time she went there, they stopped her and read her ID card all over again. On one Christmas shopping trip, she told me she was stopped no fewer than three times, and *then* a fourth guard, Patrick, started giving her a particularly hard time. As she studied Patrick, she began to get the drift. Carla was an excellent lipreader and, because she had lost her hearing long after acquiring speech, her speech was nearly perfect. Patrick just couldn't accept the fact that she was deaf. He acted like a man who wasn't going to let himself be fooled. He was going to call Carla's bluff.

I sympathized fully. The young woman was on a *shopping trip*, for heaven's sake, and suddenly she was facing a tangle of distrust and confusion that was keeping her from doing what she'd come there to do. But worse than that, she was suddenly on trial, and the burden was on her to prove her deafness to a stranger who didn't want to accept it. Exhausting! She struggled to no avail and finally blew her top. With her friend and little Questor, she stomped off. Not until they reached the car did the friend fill Carla in on a crucial bit of information.

During their altercation, it seems, another guard had called Patrick on the walkie-talkie and told him he had seen Carla whirl around in response when somebody called her across the mall. That settled it for Patrick—

this girl was pretending to be deaf, just so she could bring her dog along shopping. Here was one guard who wasn't going to fall for such shenanigans! There was no way Carla and Questor were going to get to go shopping that day.

Clearly, the guard reporting the incident to Patrick had missed the key part of the drama. A friend *had* called Carla, but below knee level Questor had responded and drawn Carla to the source of the call. By the time Carla pieced all this together she and her friend were driving off, and Carla felt herself get furious all over again. "Damn!" she snapped at her friend. "Why didn't you tell me what the guy was saying over the walkie-talkie? I was at a complete disadvantage by not knowing that!".

Oh, how familiar this was to me! The story perfectly dramatized the deaf/hearing communication problem—in every exchange there was always the danger that one essential piece of information, the one that had the potential to illuminate what was going on, or being discussed, or causing a problem, hadn't made it past the communication obstacles. In communicating with each other, deaf people have no more trouble than hearing people—and perhaps far *less* trouble, given the whole-body expressiveness of American Sign Language—conveying and picking up the tiniest nuances in meaning. It's only when the deaf and hearing are trying to communicate that the deaf are often at a disadvantage. And it's that disadvantage alone that, in the hearing world, renders deafness a "disability."

Carla's problem, though, had an extra wrinkle to it. Deafness is generally regarded as an "invisible disability"—there's no wheelchair or white cane to advertise its presence. The only real signal to hearing people that a person is deaf comes if that person has "deaf speech,"

speech learned through a painfully long, unimaginably difficult course of oral training without benefit of hearing the spoken word. But Carla gave no such clue to her disability. She had mastered both sides of the oral communication process—lipreading and speaking—to the point where her deafness was undetectable to the hearing. And yet, it was there. Having to *prove* it—in essence, having to prove *who she was* to perfect strangers who challenged her on the point—was the ultimate insult.

At the time of her shopping trip that insult was certainly nothing new to Carla, but it was not less aggravating for being commonplace. Carla told me of another instance that scraped even more directly on her nerves, as she was on a first date with a young man she liked a lot. They went to a restaurant with Questor, and wouldn't you know it, the waiter ordered them to take the dog out.

"He's a working dog," Carla told him. "I'm deaf and he is my signal dog." She handed over the ID card, but to no avail. It was clear that her perfect speech was defeating her purpose—the waiter just didn't believe she was deaf. He narrowed his eyes and then he did the unthinkable—he covered his mouth with his hand before continuing the conversation. From his narrowed eyes above his hand, Carla could see that he expected her to hear every word he said.

"This is outrageous!" she told him angrily. "Would you take away a blind person's cane and make it sit outside? As a matter of fact, I wouldn't eat here if you *gave* me the meal." The awful thing for Carla was that her date, a passive sort of guy, just couldn't understand what all the fuss was about. He didn't understand the full force of the waiter's insult and he clearly wished she'd just take Questor outside and settle down for a nice, quiet, friendly meal. So much for the date—and so much for the insensitive, passive young man.

Lots of Carla's stories had a similar edge to them. Whereas life with Chelsea was proving smooth as silk for Anne and me, Questor's presence often created almost enough trouble among hearing people to cancel out the benefit of his signal services. One awful airport story had me apprehensive when she told me about it—she was stopped on her way through security and to the boarding area of her plane no fewer than *six* times! And each stop was its own kind of nightmare, not only because it delayed her but also because it drew attention to her in a crowded public place. Several of the guards refused to be satisfied with the ID card and actually got her angry, making an instant minidrama for the other passengers to observe with interest as they waited their turn. Embarrassing? You bet. Who wants to be the center of attention when you're trying to work out a snafu in communications with somebody who doesn't speak your language? How to turn a routine travel arrangement into a three-ring circus, pronto.

Some time later, I passed through the same airport with Chelsea and had absolutely no problem. In comparing our experiences after that, Carla and I tried to account for the discrepancies.

"For one thing," Carla signed to me, "Questor's so small—not commanding, like Chelsea. People have a lot of trouble understanding the concept of working dog when they look at Questor—he just doesn't impress people as competent."

"Yes, I think that's right," I told her. "In the same way they can't exactly believe that you're deaf because of your highly developed oral skills, they can't believe that Questor's smart and practical. Seems like two instances of the same kind of prejudice—the tyranny of appearances. In fact, I bet appearances have even more to do with it. When people look at you they see a pretty, casual sort of young student. I bet those guards in the airport thought you were a rebel teenager just out to break the rules. In fact, I think that impression might account for a lot of your troubles."

"You men!" she answered. "All you have to do is look busy and determined and people make way for you—you and your fancy lady friend, Chelsea!"

Well, not quite. But people did seem to get the picture faster. Spreading the word on working dogs just wasn't a problem for me around Fresno. In fact, many people seemed delighted with the concept and took the time to stop and engage in conversation about the work and, of course, about Chelsea herself. As I had found with Lox, Chelsea very often served as a bridge with people who might never have dared broach any other subject with a deaf person. Many of the people who stopped to talk with me about Chelsea were women, but occasionally men would stop too, and after a while I started realizing that the men who stopped most were generally of a sewn-up type who ordinarily don't express their feelings.

Time after time, these fellows would begin to tell *me* dog stories—from their youth, or from their current family lives—and it would again reveal to me how deep is the connection between the canine and the human world. Dogs can touch people in profound ways, and can touch them in places that remain tightly guarded in interactions between humans. For people who already have a deep appreciation for the capacity of dogs to reach across species lines, seeing a working dog like Chelsea can be a moving experience. The work relationship gave a dimension to the dog/human interaction that few people, except perhaps sheepherders and hunters, have the chance to observe for themselves. It sometimes came to me as I went about with Chelsea how hard it would be to receive from a human being the help she gave me so freely and eagerly!

One particularly nice example of Chelsea bridging the gap between species occurred when I went to visit my elderly Uncle Wallace in a nursing home in Long Beach. I visited Uncle Wallace often, whenever I was in his town. His memory was very shaky and I knew he might not recognize me, but I was pretty sure his wife, my Aunt Grace Augusta, would be there to remind him of who I was. But when I arrived she was not at the home, and I was faced with the problem of explaining to a very blankfaced Wallace who I was, how I fit into his family, and what the dickens I was doing visiting *him*. Without much hope, I began to trace the considerable ins and outs of our mutual family tree, but—as I knew before I began—Wallace couldn't follow my speech and was getting tired trying. For long minutes we sat across from each other smiling blankly, he with a puzzled cast to his brow, I wondering what to do next. Then I had a brainstorm—I signed to Chelsea to put her paw and head on Wallace's knee.

"Oh! Yes!" cried Wallace. Confusion had disappeared and a big smile spread across his face. "Yes! You're *Paul*, Dunbar's boy! How *are* you?" Chelsea had obviously made a much greater impression than I had on our previous visits!

Slowly, we began to run across other working dogs in Fresno. Besides Questor, there was Nibbles, the companion of a visually impaired English professor at the university. This lady often visited a park Chelsea and I frequented—however, to her the park was known as Nibbles's Park while at our house we called it Chelsea's.

Some good friends of ours, Mel and Sharon, had obtained a signal dog before we did, from a center in Massachusetts. Just before they traveled there to do their boot camp, they were informed that the dog assigned to them was a German shepherd by the name of Kelly. "Kelly!" they both exploded. "But that's preposterous!" No German dog of theirs was going to be saddled with an Irish name. Upon meeting their dog, they racked their brains for a name that seemed to suit him and finally came up with a lovely one, Meine Ohren, which means "my ears" in German. It took the dog a while to make the switch, but the deed was accomplished, and the name is not only pretty and pleasing but helpful too in conveying understanding to hearing people about the signal dog's role.

Roxanne, a happy-go-lucky friend of ours, works in a small medical data exchange center in Illinois as a computer operator. She suddenly came up against the need for a signal dog at work, twice finding herself alone on a completely deserted floor. In both cases, the company had had a fire drill and all employees had vacated the premises, forgetting to alert Roxanne. The consequences, had the drill been real, were so ghastly to contemplate that Roxanne quickly arranged for a dog to be trained and sent to her from Texas. The dog who arrived was Star, a thirty-five-pound mutt with a fierce commitment to the work.

Roxanne's mother could attest to that fierceness. Over Christmas on Roxanne's first visit to her house with the dog, Star responded to the mother's alarm clock, rushing down the hall to wake her up. But Mom wasn't ready to get up and used the snooze alarm. Ten minutes later Star responded to the alarm again, and again Mom rolled over and went back to sleep. On the third ring, Star ran down the hall and bit the mother's nose. Not the CCI approach to getting a job done, but effective in its way.

Our friends Nancy and Steve had an Australian cattle dog named Gala. Gala was trained at CCI and, unlike many other canine visitors to our house, is very refined and worldly. It wasn't long after Gala and Chelsea met that they became fast friends. You could say that they had a lot in common and that each understood what the other was about, having shared the same alma mater.

Gala is the more independent dog of the two and Chelsea tends to look up to her and follow her wherever she goes. She is always in a playful mood and willing to join her in any adventure, but Gala is a very serious sort, not always open to Chelsea's unfailing gregariousness.

Steve and Nancy are constantly exchanging dog stories with us, and restaurant stories in particular, since restaurant personnel have proved, understandably, to be the most sensitive to the presence of dogs. I always loved picturing these friends and Steve's father, accompanied by Gala, awaiting their table at a four-star Newport Beach restaurant. When the headwaiter, with his nose in the air, began to protest Gala's presence, Steve's father lifted his nose at an angle to match and simply remarked, "Surely you're not thinking of refusing service to a ten-thousand-dollar dog." The answer, after a pause, must have been "certainly *not*," for they were quickly shown their table.

A less happy outcome took place in a local restaurant. When the restaurant manager came to Nancy and Steve's table to tell them "no dogs," Steve handed over the ID card and politely explained the situation. The man simply refused to be impressed. "No dogs, period." "But this is unlawful," my friends protested. *"No dogs."* "And what do you do when blind people come

in?" Steve asked with great annoyance. The answer:
"They tie their dogs up outside just like everybody
else." A few days later, after a communication from
their lawyer, the restaurant owner, terribly ashamed of
and apologetic at his employee's behavior, sent Steve
and Nancy a check in compensation. But the ruined
evening, which had been planned as a special dinner
out, could never be replaced.

In that regard, Anne and I hit upon quite an effective
retort when asked to leave a local Chinese restaurant
because of Chelsea. The waitress was very agitated at
the sight of our dog curled up quietly under the table
and refused to serve us. Beforehand, however, we had
watched her taking the order from a distraught family
whose nerves were being shattered by their crying baby.
In fact, everybody in the restaurant was eyeing the very
red, very upset little baby. "Look," I asked the waitress
when she made her irritable complaint. "Would you
rather be serving us, with our very quiet dog curled up
at our feet, or another family with a crying baby?" For
a moment I thought the waitress was going to insist that
we leave, but she saw our point and rewarded us with
a big welcome smile.

The introduction of telecaption decoders in the early
1980s revolutionized the lives of the deaf. Now, with
the TV hooked to a decoder that makes subtitles visible
on screen, we could enjoy a great many television programs. In the old days we had to rely solely on the body
language of the actors and the sequencing of the action
to get a sense of what was going on—and that usually
meant we could really get the gist of only the most boring, most action-packed, and least subtle shows. Nowadays, we have lots of closed-captioned films for the
VCR as well as closed-captioned television programs,
so we usually prefer renting a movie or watching TV to

going out to the theater. Sometimes, though, when the film seems right and we don't want to wait for it to come out on tape, Anne and I go out for a night to a movie theater.

Our friends invited us to join them to see *E.T.*, and we readily agreed, assuming from the publicity that the film would be full of action and easy to follow. We had to sit—and sleep—through another feature first, but we hoped the wait would be worth it. Our mistake! *E.T.* begins with some action but quickly settles down into talk, talk, talk. Chelsea, at my feet, settled back down for a nap along with us.

I must have drifted into a deeper sleep than I thought, because I was totally disoriented when I awoke to feel Chelsea's paws dancing on my knees in agitation. Wait—where was I, what was going on? It was pitch black and Chelsea was jumping around in the tiny space by my feet, very upset. Now I felt even more confused—someone behind me was pounding on my back! To the folks around me in the audience, it probably seemed an eternity before I finally figured out what was going on. Something had happened on the screen—later I learned that a little girl had screamed her brains out at her first sight of E.T.—and Chelsea had been terribly alarmed. Apparently she made no distinction between a real child screaming and a film image of a child screaming. From the state Chelsea was in it was clear that she wanted me to know that something was very, very wrong. I had to pull myself together and urge a very upset, nervously panting Chelsea up the aisle and out of the theater, wishing I could explain to the hundreds of annoyed patrons just what I had thought I was doing by bringing my dog to the movies anyway. That was probably a movie experience very few of them forgot, punctuated as it was by five minutes or so of her nervous panting while I slowly got the picture!

It wasn't the first time I had been embarrassed in front of a crowd. When things are going perfectly with Chelsea there's nothing I like better than to show off her regal behavior in public, and I often bring her to class or to a lecture I'm giving, where she curls up unobtrusively and conducts herself with utter composure. But if things go wrong, I'm mortified. Who doesn't hate looking up to find all eyes upon him without knowing why?

The Fresno Deaf Church is part of a larger hearing church, and deaf congregants have access there to both hearing and deaf services. At the hearing services in the main sanctuary there is a front portion reserved for the deaf and an interpreter stands in front of the deaf congregation. So while the hearing worshipers are bowing their heads in prayer, we sit with our heads up watching the interpreter. Nor do we hold up our hymn books when hymns are being sung. We keep our hands free in order to sign the hymns. There is a fluid beauty in seeing a group render a song or hymn in sign language, and an even more satisfying aesthetic in being part of such a group. Nowhere, I think, is the inherent loveliness of signing more clear. And nowhere are words and movement more effectively merged.

I once came late to a service accompanied by Chelsea and sneaked into the deaf section at the front very carefully. Everyone was deep in prayer—the hearing people all had their heads bowed; those in the deaf pews were raptly attentive to the interpreter. As I crept into a place at the end of the pew, Chelsea seemed to explode with alarm, and suddenly I was looking down the throat of a very upset, very intimidating German shepherd. Seems a blind man with his guide dog had been shown to the pew near the deaf section, by mistake. While Chelsea quivered and huddled as far away as she could, the other dog continued to go crazy—barking uncontrollably and pulling at his harness. This could have happened anywhere—on a bus, in a shopping center, even on the street. But the fact that it happened in church, among hundreds of contemplative people worshipping in silence, or relative silence, made the whole thing a sort of theater piece: people all around us were first startled and then scared out of their wits at the prospect of an all-out dogfight. Chelsea, though, refused to participate, and eventually the other man calmed his dog down.

While the incident unrolled, I was much too involved to realize that the church had suddenly been filled with the horrendous noise of furious barking. But once others described the din and I understood that we had been the source of an ungodly racket in the quiet church, I suffered an embarrassment that took days to fade.

Carla had a little story to offer along this same line. She often took Questor to her classes, and in one course the professor tended to drone and drone. It wasn't until the very end of the semester that a hearing classmate sent the message to Carla via an interpreter: "Hey, do you know your dog snores?" Apparently Questor was expressing the buried wishes of most of Carla's classmates by loudly sawing logs throughout the professor's endless lectures.

As our first year with Chelsea headed into the holiday season, we had a chance to see another side of Chelsea's personality: resignation at hustle and bustle she clearly would just as soon live without. Halloween in particular tried her patience, for she was called upon to signal that someone was at the door not just once, not twice, but maybe fifteen or twenty times an hour! But even on that first Halloween, she didn't let her dignity get ruffled. She simply stopped going to the door after the first eight or ten rings of the doorbell. Instead, she would walk to the window and eyeball the little witches and goblins assembled on the porch, sigh, and walk back to curl up by the woodstove. Puzzled, I mentioned to Kaye, Chelsea's breeder, that Chelsea seemed to give up her responsibility for the night. "It's the repetitiveness of the task," Kaye explained. "The boring nature of doing the same thing over and over. She's too smart to handle it well and probably perceives it as some sort of punishment." This only confirmed my idea of Chelsea as a dog of dignity.

When the Thanksgiving season rolled around and we had a large party, we placed a note on the door asking our friends not to pet the working dog. Chelsea seemed to resign herself to the fact that the house had been turned over to strangers for the evening. She simply made it her job to keep Anne or me within her line of sight all evening long.

One evening close to Christmas, Chelsea led us to the door when she heard something unusual. When we opened the door, Anne and I smiled broadly but darted a look at each other that said privately, "Oh, no, the carolers." It was a no-win situation that we faced every year. Did we throw cold water on the group by stopping them in their first song to let them know we were deaf and couldn't enjoy their music? Or did we simply let them go through the three or four carols they always sang to us while we stood smiling in our doorway, pretending to love the songs?

I was never comfortable with pretending—it was too much like trying to pass for hearing, an impulse some deaf people have who cannot accept the facts of who they are. So once I did interrupt the carolers and try to explain the situation to them. But this only made things worse. It had taken me a song or two to decide to interrupt, and they clearly felt like fools at having sung two carols to a couple who couldn't hear them. I tried to ease the situation by offering to teach them how to sign "Merry Christmas and a Happy New Year," and they welcomed the diversion, but the actual lesson seemed more trouble than it was worth. Now, with Chelsea, Anne and I stood at the door and once more tried to figure out what to do.

Funny, though. We missed our chance to stop the first carol and Chelsea sat absolutely rapt. She was at her most attentive, with her back at a sharp angle and her ears pointed straight up. Did Chelsea have a secret love for music that we—and perhaps she—had known nothing about? She certainly seemed to be enjoying the singing, and we had the pleasure of watching her delightful involvement. For the first time, Anne and I felt it unnecessary to solve the problem of the carolers. We all nodded and waved at each other and the carolers moved on down the block. Chelsea had her private tastes and pleasures, just like the rest of us, and it had been a treat to see one revealed so unexpectedly as she sat entranced by the sounds we couldn't hear.

CHAPTER 6

Travels with Chelsea

FROM time to time I'm asked to give a workshop, present a paper, or attend a conference in another city, and having Chelsea with me on such a trip not only increases my pleasure but eases me of certain concerns—hotel fires, for instance, or emergency phone calls in the middle of the night. It's my impression that many travelers have these same concerns, and it may be that traveling unleashes worries like picnics draw ants. But deafness adds a little edge to these matters—what if you're on the twentieth floor and the smoke alarm goes off in the middle of the night? It's true that hearing people *might* sleep through the alarm and ensuing commotion, might even sleep through repeated poundings on their door. But for deaf people the likelihood of that "might" goes up in direct proportion to the percentage of hearing loss, and what may for some people be an anxious worry becomes, for someone deaf like me, a practical matter to be dealt with.

Enter Chelsea. She may have had her moment of existential *angst* in contemplating the unbounded universe when we took her camping, but she was and is always up for a trip, preferably one requiring airplane travel. People seem to imagine that taking Chelsea on a plane is horribly complicated, but properly prepared for, travels with Chelsea are easy and bring out her best traits.

Both as a Belgian sheepdog intent on seeing her charges to their destination and as a highly trained signal dog awaiting her next command, Chelsea's at her sharpest on a trip.

Granted, she's another traveler to pack for. If we're going on a short trip, I fill her backpack with dog food, heartworm pills, plastic sandwich bags (for janitorial purposes—you slip them on your hand like a glove, then turn them inside out around the objectionable item and dispose of bag and item together), tennis ball (for recreational exercise), brush, and plastic bowl. Thus, Chelsea carries her own luggage. It's easy to see from the reactions of the guards at the X-ray stations, once they figure out what the backpack is all about (and some never do), which ones are dog lovers and which ones aren't. Those defenders of the gates, whose expressions are usually so neutral as they survey the luggage going in, can't seem to suppress their smiles or grimaces when they understand that this four-legged creature is to be passed into passenger realm—unlike poor Lox, who was boxed up, stored with the luggage, and flown off who knows where.

On longer trips I pack dog food in individual plastic bags and put them in my suitcase. Anyone opening the suitcase tends to view these bags with immediate suspicion—ten million dollars worth of exotic drugs in kibble form?—though, again, dog lovers all recognize animal feed.

The absolute number one (excuse the pun) command upon which Chelsea's sophisticated travel habits rest is the wonderful CCI command "better go now," the one that means "This is your last chance to perform your natural duties for at least four hours, so do it now, right here." Many of my friends have simply refused to believe that this magical command could really work and have demanded to be on hand for the pretrip preparation. I take Chelsea to a suitable ivy patch or dirt pile and sign "better go now." Knowing she'll have a long wait for the next chance, Chelsea starts to work on the task right away. If she doesn't have to go or she's done, she sits down and looks directly into my eyes. The message is clear: "I'm done and am ready to leave."

Onlookers can't get over the performance. I once glanced up while Chelsea was going on command in literally the only appropriate place I could find in a downtown area of a city—a tiny pile of sand at a building site—to see a whole line of hard-hat workers watching us with amazed expressions. They were probably even more astounded to see me bend down and clean up with my inside-out baggie, but I didn't look back to check!

When we are preparing to fly long distances, we have a procedure that Chelsea doesn't like at all but that is necessary to keep her comfortable. On the night before the plane trip I calculate the number of hours before take-off and the length of the complete flight. Based on this formula, I decide when to begin withholding food and water from Chelsea so she will not need to urinate or defecate from the minute we enter the airport until we reach our destination. We give the "better go now" command sign right outside the terminal and then proceed with confidence.

But Chelsea hates being kept from water and her mischief comes out as a result. As soon as she sees the luggage being prepared, she knows we're going away and shows terrific enthusiasm. Then, after I have made my calculations, I signal the beginning of the water fast by giving her a few sips and then putting all three of her water bowls away. She seems to get the message from this ritual, but sometimes during the evening she pretends she needs to go outside so she can have a quick drink from the backyard swimming pool. So we usually follow her out or watch her from the door, highly amused at the glances she throws back to us as she sniffs around the yard, hoping in vain we'll go back inside so she can sneak over to the pool for a quick one. Whenever we've caught her at it, she's run back into the house and sat in the corner—her conscience is amazingly strong and I'm sure it's what keeps her on the wagon.

Who's to say, though, how many times Chelsea has outsmarted us on this one? When Chelsea's whiskers started coming in white, Anne wondered whether this was the result of drinking chlorinated water.

On the plane we always reserve bulkhead seats, where there's a little more floor room for Chelsea. She immediately curls up and makes herself comfortable for the entire trip. On nearly every flight, the same little scenario unfolds: the stewardess mistakes Chelsea's backpack for a piece of hand luggage, opens the door to the overhead rack, leans down to pick it up, and, discovering that it's attached to a rather substantial living creature, jumps back in confusion, saying, "Oh, my goodness . . . oh, I beg your pardon . . . how on earth did he get on the plane?" Chelsea is so dark she generally fades into a dark carpet, and most planes seem to be carpeted in dark colors.

Very few passengers notice Chelsea either, since she boards close to our sides and remains calm and unobtrusive. But she didn't begin her flying days so matter-of-factly and had to become used to plane flight. During her first few flights she showed a lot of concern about the engine noises and other sounds, rising up from the floor and putting her paws on our laps to alert us and to scour our faces for clues. We would pat her and reassure her that she could return to the floor. Now, a seasoned flyer, she stays calm through the commotion of boarding, the revving up of the engines, and the resounding takeoffs. I've found, too, that her own undisturbed dignity in flying through turbulent air serves as a model for me to imitate. I tend to become very nervous at such moments, but it soothes me to contemplate Chelsea's supreme disregard of the fact that we are bouncing violently through the air in a big metal tube five miles above the ground.

One thing that did upset Chelsea's composure during many of those first trips was the crying of a baby. She clearly found it hard to suppress her strong desire to check on a distressed baby, and it took us a long time to teach her that the infant she heard wailing was fine. She would paw my lap and then move on to Anne, hoping for more understanding. Anne would then get up and speak to the parents for a few minutes to respond to Chelsea's distress by showing her that the problem was being handled and was no longer hers. Then she would come back to reassure Chelsea again. It took a few flights, but Chelsea did finally accept the fact that the parents of a crying baby could probably handle the situation without her assistance. We didn't mind Chelsea's persistence in this matter, though. It demonstrated Chelsea's participation should we ever decide to have children.

Getting Chelsea adjusted to the experience of flying was the simple side of traveling. What took more patience, and some ingenuity, was convincing certain airport personnel that Chelsea had a legal right to board the plane. We have flown through at least fifteen airports, and for the most part have had no trouble explaining Chelsea's role and legal status. But in one city, which shall remain nameless here, we ran into a brick wall. The airport guards' refusal to allow Chelsea through, even after being shown the proper documentation, was inexcusable in an informed metropolitan center, and I want to put it on the record here—along with Carla's similar experience—in the hope of reducing the chances of it ever happening again.

It's a small thing really—a guard at the boarding gate blocked our way to board the plane and wouldn't budge. The seconds were ticking away toward takeoff, and we handed him our ID card, assuming we'd be passed through.

No go. He'd have to have us talk to his superior. Another barrier. That man would have to have us wait while he talked to *his* superior. The head security guard, a huge, lazy-looking man, took his time and settled himself for a long conversation, leaning back against the corridor wall with his arms crossed. "I am hard-of-hearing and my husband is deaf," Anne said, repeating what she had told the other guards. "I read lips so please talk slowly."

The man wiped his nose on his sleeve several times and then told us he would *never* let a dog through security lines, he didn't care *where* it had gone to school. We handed him the ID card and he held it upside down and looked it over, and then handed it back, saying, "Sorry, that won't do. No dogs."

We were sweating—time was passing and we were trying to converse over the barrier of deafness with a towering idiot who had a reading problem. We looked at each other and tore off down the hall toward the airline management desk. Chelsea probably couldn't believe her luck—one minute we were standing motionless with irritation and suspense, the next we were flying down the hall faster than we'd ever run in any game of fetch.

The woman in the manager's office was instantly responsive and steered us through the process to the boarding gate. As we passed the initial security guard, he scowled with displeasure at seeing Chelsea passed through. On his face I read the message, "This is the first and last time I will ever let that animal through this gate."

Sure enough, one year later, on another trip through this same airport, we faced the same problem again. Even before we left for the airport Anne became very nervous about the possibility of trouble, and my mother, who could see Anne was petrified, advised us to take a very radical approach should we run into trouble: "Just play deaf and dumb, Paul. You'll see. This is an opportunity to do a little playacting and take advantage of the bigotry you're usually fighting." Coming from my mother, who was a central inspiration in my education and independence, this advice really shocked me.

"I can't do that, Mother," I protested. "I've spent my whole life working to convince the public that I'm alert and smart, and here you are telling me I should act stupid and helpless and play into these guards' games."

"Well, just keep it in mind," she told me. "Some people just can't stand having reality contradict their own private ideas about how things are. In this case, maybe if you go along with their idea that deaf people are dumb and helpless you'll encounter less resistance."

I just plain hated the idea, but Anne was all for it. We decided to keep it in mind, with Anne hanging back to observe while we scoped out the scene. After all, nothing had really happened yet. Maybe we were making something out of nothing.

I went forward through the whole routine of removing Chelsea's stuff and putting it up for inspection when there they were—two guards rushing up to me yelling, "No dogs! No dogs!" Okay, Mother, I said to myself silently. We'll see how this goes. It went completely against my nature to ignore people who were trying to get my attention, since it had always been a matter of pride to respond to people quickly when they spoke to me. But I simply kept moving slowly, ploddingly, through the inspection routine, and when I couldn't ignore the guards another second I simply raised my finger in the gesture that means "one second."

And then I just went through, ignoring everybody and everything. I picked up the backpack from the conveyor belt and strapped it onto Chelsea while the guards surrounded me, energetically trying to get my attention. I could sense a growing commotion, but simply kept my face to my work.

Now one of the guards jumped into my range of vision and, with his hand bobbing this way and that, seemed to be trying to fingerspell. Deaf people who need to fingerspell something in the midst of signing in American Sign Language keep the hand still in front of the chest, but this man's hand, working like crazy, was flitting around like a buzzing fly. But I finally got it— the letters "I-D."

Ah, so the fellow wants to see the card that was so readily spurned last time. I guessed I could grant him the satisfaction of getting through to me—he had definitely worked on it. I handed him the card and after reading it carefully, front and back, he waved me through and on toward the gate. I plodded along with Chelsea, still playing deaf and dumb, but inside I was marveling at the good sense of my mother. She had raised two deaf sons in a time when the public's understanding of deafness was often close to nil in some places. She must have put in a significant amount of time thinking out strategies for getting around ignorance.

Anne trailed me onto the plane and told me what had happened. Once the guards started to yell at me, she said, all passengers in line froze and the whole scene became a spectacle. As I continued on my oblivious way, the level of hollering rose to a hysterical pitch, and one man stepped out of the crowd of passengers to confront the guards. "Good Lord, man, can't you see that this young fellow is deaf? Can't you see this is a working dog with him? For heaven's sake, dogs like this are to go with the owner on the plane. Ask the man for an identification card and you'll see what I'm telling you is true." It took a while for his words to penetrate the crazy uproar, but he kept at it, explaining that he would show one of the guards how to fingerspell "I-D."

Later, Anne and I went to this assertive guy to thank him for his help. He knew American Sign Language, had worked with deaf children, and knew just how ignorant or confused the general public can be about deafness. It took someone with his experience to come up with a solution to a problem that could have made all the passengers in line, not just us, miss their plane connections.

Another incident on another trip demonstrated the public's misunderstanding in a more genteel but perhaps more bizarre way. We were staying in a charming, cozy little bed-and-breakfast in Seattle, where we had gone to visit old friends. The friends, in making the reservations, had explained to the proprietor about Chelsea, and she welcomed the idea of having her come to stay.

The place was small and quaint, at the top of a very steep hill. Inside it was filled with China dolls and all sorts of little objects. It was beautiful but perhaps just the tiniest bit claustrophobic—and that feeling was intensified for me by the proprietor's constant, minute attentions. We had been pleased to find we were the only guests but I soon began wishing this attentive lady had other people to care for. She woke us up very early on our first morning to ask us if Chelsea didn't need to go outside. We explained that she would let us know when she needed to be let out. During breakfast, the lady hovered around us, asking where Chelsea was and then forgetting what we told her, that she was curled up under our feet. There was an anxious quality to this lady's concern, and I ascribed it to her worry about her lovely house and the things in it. But during our conversations she also seemed terribly worried about how we were going to make our way around the city. "But how will your dog know where to go if she has never been here before?"

"Oh, we'll figure it out. Nothing to worry about. We've got our maps and everything."

"Ahh," said the woman, looking puzzled. "Ahh, good. Well if I can help at all. . . ."

Slowly, as the lady continued to hover, we started to sense what the trouble was. At the table the next morning, after asking us about our day, the lady confirmed our suspicions.

"You have such a beautiful city," Anne told her. "We've loved sightseeing around Seattle."

"Sightseeing?" said the lady. "But I thought . . ."

"Oh, yes, we're avid sightseers," I told her, with Anne repeating what I said and signed, since the woman was unable to understand my speech. "We love to walk through any new city we go to and see the sights from the streets."

She seemed dumbfounded and then self-conscious. She buried her confusion by offering Chelsea a plate full of bacon and eggs, which we gently refused.

"Wait a minute," I said. "Is it that you think Anne and I can't see?"

She smiled nervously and looked away, then looked back, then drew in her eyebrows and admitted, "Well, yes."

"Oh, no," said Anne. "I'm hard-of-hearing and Paul is deaf. But we can see fine."

"Oh, oh, oh," said the lady, shaking her head. She was clearly embarrassed. "But your dog! Oh, dear, I guess I was a little confused."

All this time she had thought we were blind!

We had talked of being deaf, had explained Chelsea's role, had used the word *deaf* continually, but this was one of the people who grow up with a misconception of deafness so deep that, as my mother had put it, reality can't touch it. I had run into this before in question-and-answer sessions following my public presentations. Often someone would ask, "Do you drive a car?" Knowing what was coming, I would answer yes, only to have that conversation-stopper thrown at me: "But how can you drive if you can't see what's coming?" As patiently as I could, I would explain that I was deaf, not blind, hoping I would see the brightened expression indicating that the confused person has experienced an "Aha!" These interchanges always depressed me, since they meant that at least one person in the audience had been sitting through an hour-long presentation on deafness without ever being struck by the facts I had been painstakingly laying out.

Happily, this confusion seems to be pretty much limited now to people over sixty. In the younger generations ignorance is giving way to a real interest in deafness and an enthusiasm for American Sign Language. Before the general loosening up that occurred throughout the culture beginning in the late 1960s, deafness, along with a lot of other "differences," was locked firmly away in the closet—unacknowledged, undiscussed, and completely misunderstood.

This buttoned-up approach to deafness, which often led families to feel ashamed of their deaf children, was harbored within my own extended family, although I didn't realize it until I was an adult and had published my first book, on young deaf children, in 1982. At this time my father's sister, my aunt Grace Augusta, and her husband Wallace, my father's best friend—the same Wallace that Chelsea and I visited in the nursing home—revealed, not to me but to my *mother*, that their grandniece, Melinda, was deaf. So at the age of thirty-three I learned for the first time that I had a cousin who was deaf—and a teacher of the deaf, as I learned when I met her a year later.

What a shame, my brother Dunbar and I thought. Imagine all the sharing of information that could have taken place at a time when information on deafness was at a premium. The educational choices parents had to make were difficult then, as now, but without free-flowing information and supportive, stimulating dialogue, parents and their deaf children had little to help them through the maze. My parents, having raised two deaf sons, would have been a wonderful resource for Melinda and her family, but never was a word said. These relatives had been brought up in a very different era from our own today. There was no way around it: deafness made them ashamed.

This closeted thinking led directly to the sort of misconception that was addling our hotel proprietor. I've run across myriad variations on the theme—that deaf people are mentally retarded; that deafness is the result of brain damage; that deaf people are emotionally unbalanced and should be institutionalized; that it's illegal for deaf people to have children. I'm philosophical by now and purposefully patient in clarifying the truth wherever I can. But I must say I find it refreshing and enjoyable to talk to people who have some basic understanding of deafness, who have allowed themselves to confront the subject without shame or embarrassment clouding the issue, and who can appreciate the positive things about deaf culture—such as American Sign Language and the sense of community it fosters, the beautiful deaf performing arts movement, and the many satisfactions of finding ways over and around a truly formidable obstacle to easy communication.

It's not always the older folks, though, who mistake the deaf for the blind. Anyone, I guess, can make a mistake, and Chelsea's presence alone can trigger misunderstanding. For example, in Berkeley once on a beautiful Sunday morning, Chelsea and I were strolling back to my brother Dunbar's house from my favorite bakery. There's a kind of feel on Sundays in Berkeley sometimes that makes you feel you might never have been so happy—I was just floating along with my dog, enjoying the street scene and the smell of fresh bread. I had just crossed a busy boulevard and became stranded by traffic on the island in the middle, but I wasn't in a hurry and was patiently waiting for a break in the traffic when I felt somebody grab my arm. Good grief! I thought. A woman was clutching me tightly with one arm, holding the other with her hand up to stop traffic, and literally dragging me across the street. Chelsea began to jump around, barking furiously, but was dragged along too—perhaps thinking we were being kidnapped. I caught a glimpse of the determined woman's face as she stared down the oncoming traffic and recognized her as the one who ran the flower stall on the corner. I finally got it as we stumbled up the curb. She had left her post at the flower stand to "rescue" a blind man and his dog from the deadly traffic swooping past the island on both sides.

On the sidewalk once again, this Good Samaritan hugged me, smiled at me, and waited for me to thank her for saving my life.

Which I did. She had obviously been concerned about me, had made a sincere effort to help, and was pleased to have been able to be of service. I smiled back at her and squeezed her hand, hoping it had helped make her Sunday to rescue a blind man in distress.

In Seattle, though, things could have gotten complicated had we not cleared up that particular misunderstanding. Luckily, simply by being there, Chelsea helped the hotel proprietor recover from her embarrassment. When she realized what had happened the good woman dove down under the table to stroke Chelsea's coat. When she surfaced she was composed, and then we were all in a position to understand each other quite a bit better—she with a new light on deafness and we with a sudden insight into her overbearing attentions to our every need.

From Seattle we flew out to Victoria, British Columbia. The plane for that flight turned out to be a little twelve-seater, and though I had been promised bulkhead seats, it turned out that the seats reserved for us were directly behind the pilot and copilot, I on one side of the aisle, Anne on the other—and Chelsea flat in the middle. I felt my heart sink as I saw that the pilot and copilot would have to step over our dog to get to their own seats—but they did so with such obvious enjoyment of her presence that the considerable anxiety I was feeling about flying in a tiny plane lifted away.

In Victoria we had a fabulous time, capped by a special evening with my old friend Robie, whom I'd met at school long, long ago, and his wife Sara. The dinner at the wonderful restaurant at the Empress Hotel, where we were staying, was to be a celebration of Anne and my ten-year wedding anniversary and my thirty-year friendship with Robie.

We dressed carefully, savoring the feeling of specialness of the evening, and took the elevator down to the restaurant for our six o'clock reservations. The headwaiter greeted us warmly and with a flourish began leading us to our table, but he stopped cold at the sight of Chelsea. I felt time freeze—what was going to happen next? Terribly uneasy, he led us back to the reservation stand and said, "I'm so sorry. I'm afraid the other guests at the restaurant may not appreciate the presence of the dog." We went through our routine and showed the ID card. "One moment," he told us and went to fetch the manager while we held our breath in suspense. Oh, dear, Anne and I said to each other silently. The last thing we wanted was a scene in which somebody might get angry. But an even worse prospect tonight was that our friends' special evening could be ruined, too.

The manager, a Mr. Chastings, was a suave young man in his twenties. He looked beautifully groomed and sophisticated, but his composure was shaken slightly when he saw Chelsea eagerly wagging her tail and smiling up at him from the plush carpet in the elegantly muted light. I was even aware of a slight expression of distaste as he came toward us with his hand outstretched and a tight, bright smile on his face.

"Would it perhaps be possible to leave your dog in your room for the evening?" he suggested, his smile a mile wide but his eyes almost pleading.

"Oh, no, not at all," I said, with Anne interpreting. "Chelsea can never be left alone in a strange place. But she is highly trained to behave quietly and calmly in restaurants. You and your patrons will never know she is here once we have been seated."

Mr. Chastings was nodding in a friendly way, but it was obvious that his mind was racing. The suspense built to a higher pitch as he excused himself, still smiling but sweating slightly now. When he returned he had a solution. "I've arranged for a special table to be set aside a bit from the main body of the restaurant so that none of the other patrons could possibly object to the presence of your dog. But there's only one thing—the table will be a bit far away from the band platform, so you might have trouble hearing the music." He caught himself in horror—I could actually see the realization hit that he was talking to four deaf people about listening to the music! For a moment I thought this worldly, sophisticated young man might even cry with embarrassment, but we all rushed to reassure him.

"We haven't come for the music, but for the wonderful food and atmosphere," I told him. "Thank you so much for arranging our special table. I'm sure it will be fine."

Relief turned Mr. Chastings's strained smile genuine and he turned to the headwaiter and asked him to show us the way.

As soon as we were seated, it was the headwaiter's turn to lose his cool. With everyone comfortably arranged, he looked around suddenly and visibly shouted in panic, "Where is that dog? Where did it go?" In his mind's eye he seemed to be imagining Chelsea sniffing her way through the sea of elegantly clad and nyloned legs, perhaps even lifting a leg of her own on a table base or two.

"She's here, she's here—under the table." The calm expression resettled itself on the man's face once again.

Three waiters served us during our seven-course

meal. The first waiter greeted us warmly and passed out the menus. Then he leaned over confidentially and said, "I hear you have a dog with you? Where is he?"

"It's a she. She's under the table between Paul's feet."

"What's her name?"

"Chelsea."

"I can't see her right now. It's too dark. Would you let the headwaiter know when you are leaving the restaurant? I'd be very pleased to meet Chelsea."

When the second waiter showed up, he said the same thing. "I hear you have a dog with you. I'd love to see her after your meal."

And the third showed the same interest.

Then, as we were enjoying our meal, out came the chef, in his cap and apron, to ask how our dinner was.

"Fantastic!" we replied. "Loved it."

He leaned over confidentially and asked, "May I see your dog?" We promised to send a message to him in the kitchen when we were ready to leave.

After two and a half hours, we were finally ready for a good, long walk. We called the headwaiter and asked him to pass the message along that we were getting ready to leave, and much to our hilarity, not three, not four, but *twelve* staff people came out of the kitchen with the chef. They and the waiters actually formed two rows for us to march through with Chelsea. I couldn't decide whether this was a collection of true and sincere dog lovers or whether the appearance of a dog in that refined atmosphere was too unusual to pass up.

Whatever the explanation, I loved seeing all those people in white beaming at my dog. All of them, remarking on her demeanor and probably thanking her under their breath for not puddling the carpet or frightening a guest, seemed to gather for the sole purpose of celebrating Chelsea's fine nature and impeccable behavior. She walked between them glowing and beaming back, just as she should have done—pleased with their attention but completely, regally, in control. I remembered my initial impression of Chelsea as a fine lady with impeccable breeding. The lady's in her element, I mused, there's no mistaking that. She's probably thinking as she walks down the aisle, "Well, finally!"

CHAPTER 7

A Walk on the Beach to a Wedding

CHELSEA might have the demeanor of a lady, but she never, never lets us forget she is a sheepdog.

Last spring we took a long walk on the beach south of Santa Cruz, toward a place called the Wedding Cove. We'd been invited to the wedding of two deaf friends, who designed their own wedding ceremony for this breathtaking natural setting. Anne, Chelsea, and I ambled along happily. A couple of dozen yards in front were our deaf friends Nancy and Steve, carrying their year-old baby—and our goddaughter—Christl. Gala, their CCI dog, trotted on a leash beside them. I let Chelsea go. She took off, prancing up to our friends ahead, circling them with a quick sniff for Gala, and then bounding back. Up and back she went, keeping a close eye on me all the while. Of course, she checked out everything on the way—shells, bunches of seaweed, abandoned sand castles, and the feet of every walker and cluster of children—her long nose scooping the sand left and right at high speed, like the spoiler on a windup racecar. Never stopping, only pausing, ranging out and coming back, eventually she closed in to circle around her extended family before trotting back to me. This pattern she continued the whole way up the beach.

"Look," I said to Anne. "She's herding. A shepherd always walks behind his flock, and his dog is supposed to run on ahead and keep the animals in a bunch. That's what she's doing. Those four," I said, pointing to our friends, "are her sheep!"

When friends and members of my family fail to walk out in front of me as she must think is right, Chelsea ranges way out to the sides, sniffing every item and person in sight, running much farther away, and returning less frequently. "Maybe when she runs out to the side she's looking for a stray sheep," I mused. There are times too when she nips me or Anne at the backs of our legs and heels—fast little bites, not very pleasant. I'm sure that's Chelsea's sheepdog way of getting her sheep to move on, pick up the pace, go where she wants us to go. When Anne has on nylon stockings, as she did now, she really hates those little nips. So we give Chelsea her leash to carry in her mouth and everyone is happy.

Chelsea has her instincts but she also has her moods, and today she was exuberant. She lifted her paws high, sometimes breaking into a run, moving to a quick left and then right. Her nose would go down, then up for a glance, then down. Her mouth was open in a concentrated pant, her tongue out extra long. Her tail wasn't wagging but flapping back and forth. Her pointed ears turned ever so slightly this way and that and she had happy feet. In our six years together, I have gotten to "read" her body language so well I can even tell if her conscience is bothering her. When her ears are down and her shoulders slope a little, she has probably been eating something forbidden. But not this day. We were both up today, excited. There was a wedding in the air!

In past times I've been on this same beach feeling very low. On those days Chelsea has sensed my mood and tried to cheer me up by prancing extra high and extra close. This is a part of what her CCI instructor calls "appropriate" behavior. In truth, it can't be taught. Certainly you can order your dog to "sit" or "stop," and if rigorously trained she'll do it. But underneath her skin there is a natural sensitivity to the occasion and what's expected of her. At another wedding, my nephew's, Chelsea lay quietly under the table while a hundred people ate and danced for four hours and then swung the couple around the hall lifted high on chairs. She knew what was happening and what we needed from her.

I call this intuition we share for each other's moods our yin and yang principle. If I'm blue, Chelsea tries to brighten my spirits with sprightly moves. On the other hand, if *she's* down—when her feet drag a little, her mouth sort of lags open, and her tail sags—I try to pep her up with a funny call and an extra pat. We do these things with each other wholly on instinct, not on command.

To be "a dutifully analytical" dog—an important CCI characteristic—an animal must not only attend to incoming sounds and differentiate significant acoustic information from nonsignificant sounds and background noise, but also integrate visual, auditory, and olfactory information into an accurate interpretation and finally a readable signal.

In order to be "reasonably protective," another CCI requirement, the dog has to be assertive, not aggressive. This means taking an active role in being on the lookout without directly going after a suspicious person. Signal dogs do not wait for commands all the time, as service dogs and social dogs are trained to do. They have a different kind of role, which includes not only keeping watch but also making decisions—"alert the master" or "let it pass."

Still, the "dutifully analytical" and "reasonably protective" dogs need both intuition and a social spirit to keep them fully engaged. For this, the perfect dog/human matchup is essential. I've always felt my match with Chelsea was the best there could be.

As I watched Chelsea weave her way down the beach I thought about the angry outburst at the motel that morning. Anne had explained carefully about the special role and privileges of a working dog. But after the girl at the front desk had disappeared into the back room to confer with the adult in charge, her mother charged out in a rage. Here was a woman who had obviously cleaned up her share of dog poop and dog hair over the years. Still, she had to abide by the law and she finally let Chelsea in. Just for fun, when we checked out the next day I left in the room a copy of a "Dear Abby" letter from a couple of years ago.

This message was sent to me by a dog lover who had seen it framed, above the registration desk, in a small hotel. And here it is:

Dogs are welcome in this hotel. We never had a dog that smoked in bed and set fire to the blankets. We never had a dog who stole our towels, played the TV too loud or had a noisy fight with his traveling companion. We never had a dog that got drunk and broke up the furniture. So if your dog can vouch for you, you're welcome, too.

My reverie was interrupted suddenly when a big, burly man stopped me in my sandy stroll. Oh, no, I thought, alarmed. This man looked angry, and he was mumbling something to me about Chelsea. I looked around for Anne, but she had walked far on ahead. What on earth could this fellow be objecting to? Chelsea hadn't even gone close to him. An emotional situation is always ridiculous and scary when I can't understand a person.

Should I pretend to understand him by smiling, nodding my head, and then walk away, telling myself, "Let it go. You're on vacation"? Or should I just shrug my shoulders, and point to my ear and say, "I'm deaf"?

As a deaf person, I often have no way of determining what is usually conveyed by the tone of voice—the mood, intention, even the level of seriousness of the message. Was this guy, who kept pointing at Chelsea, being funny or was he serious about something? He looked awfully mean and intimidating. And he mumbled. I thought I better figure out what he was saying so stiffly, his lips grinding together without forming distinct words, or he might wind up punching me in the nose.

Finally I took out a piece of paper and pencil and gave them to him. He looked lost with the paper and pencil. For a few seconds I wondered if he was illiterate.

I said, "I cannot hear you and I cannot read your lips, so please write what you want to say." On the paper he wrote, "Where did you buy the dog? It does not say L. L. Bean Dog on the backpack." Still no smile. Man, I hate people who mumble. But then I knew he was teasing me. He took the paper again to write that he wished he could find a dog like Chelsea. I was amazed to realize that this somewhat intimidating fellow was settling in for a chat. One more case of a dog warming up a human interaction.

Suddenly, though, a jeep pulled up out of nowhere and the burly man backed off as I was overtaken by commotion. Chelsea raced to my side. Anne, who had strolled out ahead, was running back toward me. Two men were in the jeep; one had a bullhorn turned in my direction. Anne was crying, "Listen, I'm hard-of-hearing and my husband is deaf. Look at our faces when you talk. Or use a pencil and paper." They couldn't hear us. Chelsea was cowering. Obviously the jeep was very loud. The face behind the bullhorn was getting redder. As the man yelled at me, he pointed at Chelsea. I waited. "Beach Patrol," I read on the door. The guy with the bullhorn was coming over, struggling with the last remnants of forced civility to rein in his anger. By now his mouth was working hard. If you can't read the lips of a mumbler, you certainly can't read the lips of a shouter, but you have no trouble telling his mood. Why was this policeman so mad at me? The shouter was pointing at Chelsea. Then I lipread "leash." By this time feisty Anne was giving the Beach Patrol boys a piece of her mind. She speaks more loudly and clearly than I, and on this occasion, perhaps inspired by the beach setting, she was using a sailor's vocabulary. The jeep patrol turned tail and ran. Anne had the last salty word, and Chelsea and I marched calmly on, now linked by our usual CCI-blue leash.

We were approaching the wedding party. I greeted the bride and felt the festivities take hold of me. Chelsea deserved a holiday, too, I felt, so I let her settle down with a group of children playing in the sand. A five-year-old girl came up and started talking to me and I sighed at the hard work in store for me. Young hearing kids are very difficult to communicate with because they have not been taught to look up into a deaf person's face or to enunciate or carefully sign. Where was Christl? I wondered, scanning the group for my little goddaughter. Now there was a child, hearing herself but with two deaf parents, with whom communication would always be a breeze.

When Nancy became pregnant two years before, the couple's CCI dog, Gala, knew immediately that something special was happening. Throughout the pregnancy, Nancy and Steve worked at refreshing Gala's memory of her child-related training, reviewing baby sounds with her with a special tape from CCI. As Nancy grew bigger. Gala became accustomed to the baby items that started appearing all over the house. Finally, one night about midnight, Nancy's water broke.

Instead of taking Gala with them to the hospital, they decided to leave her in the backyard with the sliding door a little bit open. This was hard on a working dog who had been a constant presence in their lives since boot camp. Hours later, Steve returned home to discover that Gala had vented her frustration by destroying the screen door and some of the living room furniture. To comfort her and aid in the big transition to come, Steve decided to take her back to the hospital to visit Nancy. Everyone in maternity gathered around to fuss over the dog. This helped Gala feel like part of the family again. After Nancy and Christl came home, Gala performed her normal duties well and even began alerting them to Christl's waking hours when she'd start to fuss or cry or coo.

Steve and Nancy honored Anne and me by asking us to be Christl's godparents. We attended the baptism in a small rustic church tucked away in the hills behind San Jose. In addition to family and friends, the local deaf community was there in full force, making the event quite unusual for many people in the church congregation. The Catholic priest, with the help of a sign language interpreter, wove a lovely picture of Christl in her life to come, surrounded by lots of caring people and Gala. He even mentioned the presence of Chelsea, a touch that pleased Anne and me no end.

Although the priest had had little experience with interpreters, he seemed to feel very comfortable. And he intuitively avoided the "huddling" one finds at most baptisms and weddings. Huddling is a "private party" at the altar, a circle like a football huddle that includes just the pastor, with bride and groom facing away from the congregation and excluding them. This grouping impairs the clear vision necessary for those who communicate visually. A close deaf friend of mine was married in a huddled ceremony with the interpreter outside the huddle. He had to turn away from time to time to watch the interpreter instead of reading the lips of the pastor, whom he couldn't follow. Finally, when it came time for the couple to say their vows, and to his undying embarrassment, my friend popped up with "I do" to the interpreter instead of to the bride.

All Christl's deaf friends, however, could enjoy the full spectacle of her baptism and, thanks to the accurate efforts of the interpreter, could "read" every word pronounced. The priest talked of Christl's future as a bilingual child—a hearing girl who would speak and also sign almost from birth. "How much better the world would be," he said, "if all people were as sensitive to the power and fragility of human communication as you all are." It was the first time I had ever heard an articulate person who was not a parent or a teacher of the deaf elaborate on the sensitivity of deaf people. "The deaf," he went on, "could teach us how really to talk with each other." I was deeply touched.

Now Christl was a year old and completely at ease in both the hearing and deaf worlds. I spotted her playing in the midst of the hearing children. As I watched, Anne and Nancy stepped over to her and she looked up to read their signs. The priest's sensitive and appreciative predictions seemed to be happily borne out. Her ease in both worlds was apparent.

The wedding was beginning. Against the beauty of the Pacific coastline, the deaf minister from our Fresno Deaf Church, the bride and groom, and the entire wedding party stood to face the congregation. In a regular church they would have turned their backs to us and faced the altar, but not here. The entire ceremony was conducted in sign language, and in this case a voice interpreter spoke the words for the hearing members of the audience. In this way everyone in the congregation, both deaf and hearing, was able to participate fully, and the physical movements and gestures served as a beautiful and powerful way for the bride and groom to express their love to each other openly.

Even the music was made accessible to the deaf congregants—we all took pleasure in watching the instruments being played, and the interpreter signed the lyrics in the rhythmic patterns that reflected the music. With the grace of the signing in my peripheral vision, I focused my eyes out to sea, and the waves almost seemed to match time with the signing. Then the minister began to sign again and the interpreter stepped back a little and continued voicing for the hearing people. Such moments of completely free-flowing communication with no barriers are paradise for deaf people. To us the sight of the interpreter voicing for the hearing was a dynamic reminder of how perfect the deaf world could be—and how much more fully hearing people could understand not only us deaf but each other as well. We had come a long way, I mused, since Anne and my own beach wedding fourteen years earlier.

An hour before the sun set the whole family had trekked out to the beach. After days of rain and wet weather, the

sun had just come out and the sunset promised to be
spectacular. Anne showed up with her parents in a Mid-
summer Night's Dream *dress—and barefoot (it was the
seventies, after all). Everyone surrounded my father, a
minister, with a view to the 4:00 P.M. winter gold. Anne
and I had felt it was important to my father that we listen to him directly, so we didn't use an interpreter for
ourselves. Even though his relatively unsupple lips and
truly historic long-windedness had always made it hard
for me to read his lips, we agreed to lipread for the ceremony to avoid the risk of hurting his feelings. Before
the ceremony we went over everything together, with my
older hearing brother, Dunbar, making sure we all understood each other fully. One of our close friends sign-
interpreted for our deaf friends but she stood a little off
to the left, out of our peripheral range.*

Exhilarated by the scenery of the sunset, we stood out
there on the beach and read the lips of my father. He
read his favorite passages from the New Testament, and
then all at once, unexpectedly, he stopped talking. Puzzled, I turned to Anne. Her right arm was hooked into
my left arm; her left hand held a bouquet of yellow
roses. I glanced down, and with her right hand tucked
inside my left arm she made the sign that meant "I love
you." I was surprised and pleased and guessed that
Anne and my father had cooked it up together. I kissed
Anne. My father resumed the ceremony, and ended just
before the colors of the sunset started to fade away.

At the wedding dinner I told Dunbar how thrilled I
had been with the surprise. For a second, he didn't
seem to understand. Then recognition flashed on his
face. "Oh, I see what you are saying," he said—and
thereupon he erased the magic from the part of the ceremony I most treasured. "Oh, that was an airplane!

Dad had to quit talking until the engine sounds died away."

Apparently Anne had seen me wondering, had nudged me, and had shown me the sign for an airplane! Since she was holding my arm, her hand was horizontal, not vertical. If her arm had been free she would have held her hand differently, and I would never have mistaken "airplane" for "I love you." Oh, well, I thought. No doubt more than one hearing person, besotted with love and happiness, had mistaken crazier words than "airplane" for whispered expressions of love.

Now, fourteen years later at another wedding on the beach, the minister was signing, "You may kiss the bride." I felt a tug on my sleeve and glanced down. She was signing it right this time. She too was remembering. I bent down and kissed her and flashed the ILY sign back. Chelsea leaned hard against my leg. I think "ILY" is a hand sign she picked up from us, not CCI. She was reading my sign and, very much the self-assured lady, assumed I meant it for her.